✔ KU-571-093

BANGKOK

|CONDENSED|

 rebecca turner

LONELY PLANET PUBLICATIONS
Melbourne • Oakland • London • Paris

contents

Bangkok Condensed
1st edition – September 2002

Published by
Lonely Planet Publications Pty Ltd
ABN 36 005 607 983
90 Maribyrnong St, Footscray, Vic 3011, Australia
www.lonelyplanet.com or AOL keyword: lp

Lonely Planet offices
Australia Locked Bag 1, Footscray, Vic 3011
☎ 0 8379 8000 fax 613 8379 8111
e talk2us@lonelyplanet.com.au
USA   150 Linden St, Oakland, CA 94607
☎ 510 893 8555 Toll Free 800 275 8555
fax 510 893 8572
e info@lonelyplanet.com
UK   10a Spring Place, London NW5 3BH
☎ 020 7428 4800 fax 020 7428 4828
e go@lonelyplanet.co.uk
France   1 rue du Dahomey, 75011 Paris
☎ 01 55 25 33 00 fax 01 55 25 33 01
e bip@lonelyplanet.fr
www.lonelyplanet.fr

Design Vicki Beale Maps Kusnandar, Chris Love, Adrian
Persoglia, Yvonne Bischofberger Editing Melanie
Dankel, Craig MacKenzie Cover Daniel New Publishing
Manager Diana Saad Thanks to Bruce Evans, Charles
Rawlings-Way, Chris Love, Emma Koch, Gabrielle
Green, James Hardy, Jane Thompson, LPI, Nikki
Anderson, Rowan McKinnon and Darren O'Connell.

Photographs
Photography by Richard I'Anson. Other photos by
Anders Blomqvist (p. 53) and Richard Nebesky (p. 55).

All of the photographs in this guide are available for
licensing from Lonely Planet Images:
www.lonelyplanetimages.com

Front cover photographs
Top View of the Bangkok skyline from the Chao
Phraya River (Ryan Fox)
Bottom Detail of statue at entrance of the Royal
Monastery of the Emerald Buddha at Wat Phra Kaew
(Richard I'Anson)

ISBN 1 74059 351 0

Text & maps © Lonely Planet Publications Pty Ltd 2002
Photos © photographers as indicated 2002
Printed through Colorcraft Ltd, Hong Kong
Printed in China

how to use this book

SYMBOLS

⊠ address

☎ telephone number

🚊 nearest train station

🚌 nearest bus route

🚢 nearest water transport

🚗 auto route, parking details

☺ opening hours

ⓘ tourist information

$ cost, entry charge

e email/website address

♿ wheelchair access

☗ child-friendly

✕ on-site or nearby eatery

V good vegetarian selection

COLOUR-CODING

Each chapter has a different colour code which is reflected on the maps for quick reference (eg, all Highlights are bright yellow on the maps).

MAPS

The fold-out maps inside the front and back covers are numbered from 1 to 7. All sights and venues in the text have map references which indicate where to find them on the maps; eg (3, A8) means Map 3, grid reference A8. Although each item is not pin-pointed on the maps, the street address is always indicated.

PRICES

Price gradings (eg, 100/50B) usually indicate the adult/concession entry charges to a venue. Concession prices can include senior, student, member or coupon discounts.

AUTHOR AUTHOR !

Rebecca Turner

Her first visit to Bangkok was at the tender age of nine and she left clutching a traditional Thai doll and Hello Kitty pencilcase. Over the next couple of decades, she's repeated the ritual often, except now she leaves with bulging, overweight suitcases and the taste of *kŭaytiaw phàt khîi mao* burnt into her tongue. At home in Sydney, she is trying to come to terms with the lack of Thai massages in her life.

Thanks to Andrew Burrell, Kate Burrell, Ian Crawshaw, Joe Cummings for his original Bangkok city guide research, Patrick Donohoe, Carly Hammond, Colin Kruger, Paula Kruger, Catriona Purcell, Natalie Schneider and Sally Webb.

READER FEEDBACK

Things change – prices go up, schedules change, good places go bad and bad places improve or go bankrupt. So, if you find things better or worse, recently opened or long since closed, please tell us and help make the next edition even more accurate. Send all correspondence to the Lonely Planet office closest to you (listed on p. 2) or visit e www.lonelyplanet.com/feedback.

Lonely Planet books provide independent advice. Lonely Planet does not accept advertising in guidebooks, nor payment in exchange for listing or endorsing any place or business. Lonely Planet writers do not accept discounts or payments in exchange for positive coverage of any sort.

facts about bangkok

Also known as 'The City Where Anything Goes But The Traffic', Bangkok is the modern Asian metropolis at its steamiest and most exhilarating.

Just like any good Buddhist, you have to struggle to reach enlightenment in Bangkok but when it hits you'll understand that famous Thai smile. On a bad day – when the heat, the noise and the traffic get you down – Bangkok sucks the life out of you, spits you out and throws you on the ground.

But on a good day – and there will be many – it picks you back up and places you into a world whose dominant religion is having fun, or making *sànùk* as the locals like to say. Follow their lead and carouse in bars until all hours, eat Thai food until you burst and laugh until you cry.

Though it might be hard to see beyond the smog and skyscrapers, there is a method to Bangkok's madness – and that's its Thai-ness. It reveals itself in the daily Buddhist rituals at beautiful temples, in the orchids that dangle from a longtail boat's bow as it bolts down a canal, in the gentle *wâi* greeting.

Seek out the beauty and you'll start to understand what makes this intriguing city tick.

Late evening view of the Skytrain track – your gateway to Bangkok's nightlife

HISTORY
The Thonburi Days
An early settlement at Thonburi on the western bank of Mae Nam Chao Phraya (Chao Phraya River), the opposite side to modern Bangkok's city centre, was known as Bang Makok, or Place of the Olive Plums. Thonburi grew from a fishing village to a strategic trading city in the final centuries of Ayuthaya's reign as capital of Siam. When Ayuthaya, upriver to the north, was sacked by the Burmese in 1765, Thai general Phraya Taksin proclaimed himself king and made Thonburi the new capital. But Taksin became erratic and megalomaniacal, so his ministers disposed of him, setting the scene for the foundation of the Chakri dynasty, which rules Thailand to this day.

> **Tongue-Twisting Title**
> At 26 words long, Bangkok's Thai name is a bit of a mouthful, so everyone shortens it to Krung Thep, or City of Angels. The full-length version can be translated as: 'Great city of angels, the repository of divine gems, the great land unconquerable, the grand and prominent realm, the royal and delightful capital full of nine noble gems, the highest royal dwelling and grand palace, the divine shelter and living place of reincarnated spirits'.

A New Capital Across the River
In 1782, Chao Phraya Chakri, or King Rama I, busily began preparing a new capital on the Bangkok, or eastern, side of the river – he thought it would be easier to defend against naval attack from here. A Chinese settlement on the site he fancied for the new royal palaces and government buildings was relocated to the Sampeng district, which is today's Chinatown. Ayuthaya artisans built temples, while kilometres of city walls were built by Khmer prisoners of war, who created a royal 'island', called Ko Ratanakosin, by expanding the city's canal system.

The waterways were a key element in the cycle of life in the 'Venice of the East'. Locals used the river and its web of canals for transport, as a marketplace (with the famous floating markets), for bathing and as a source of food and water. Traditional houses were built on stilts, often over the water, to avoid the flooding of the monsoon season.

The Chao Phraya River Express kicks into hyperdrive.

Modernisation

Reforms during the mid-18th and early 19th centuries took Bangkok, and Thailand, into the modern era. The reform-oriented agenda of Rama IV (1851-68), or King Mongkut, was continued by his son, Rama V (1868-1910), or King Chulalongkorn, who created the civil service, still one of Bangkok's biggest employers. Chulalongkorn created a new royal residential complex for himself and his family in Dusit, away from the traditional compound in Ratanakosin.

As motorised transport took off, Bangkok expanded in every which way with new motorways (little did they know what they were in for). The political landscape changed rapidly, too, with a bloodless coup in 1932 abruptly ending the era of absolute monarchy and ushering in a constitutional monarchy. Then in 1939 the country's official name changed from Siam to Thailand. Modernisation hiccuped during WWII, but soon enough Bangkok resumed its steady program, with canals filled in for roads and bridges built over the river. Bangkok's infamous sex industry was born during the Vietnam War days, when it was a popular R&R stop for foreign troops stationed in South-East Asia.

Political Upheaval

In the 1970s, democracy was on a shaky path – the military brutally suppressed a pro-democracy student rally in Bangkok and the country later see-sawed between civilian and military rule. But big demonstrations in 1992, calling for the resignation of the latest military dictator, saw violent street confrontations between protesters and the military near Democracy Monument, resulting in 50 deaths. After a right royal scolding from the king, the dictator resigned. Since 1992 democratically elected civilian coalitions have administered the government.

Bubbles & Spirals

Bangkok was the beating heart of one of Asia's hottest tiger economies, attracting dreamers and entrepreneurs keen to make their fortune. Modern skyscrapers tickled the skyline, and the middle and upper classes developed a taste for Western luxury goods. But in 1997, the bubble burst and the Thai currency spiralled ever downwards – people's incomes halved overnight while expats left in droves.

Bangkok Today

The economy was showing signs of recovery, after a financial restructuring, but the global economic slowdown has again put it on shaky ground. But Bangkok's bright lights and big city lure are still irresistible to the rural and working-class Thais looking to make a better life.

Jazzin' at the Palace

You're more likely to hear King Bhumibol than see him. A jazz composer and saxophonist, he jammed with Woody Herman and Benny Goodman in his younger days and his big-band-style numbers are often played on Thai radio. But when he is out and about, he's often seen cruising in a yellow vintage Rolls Royce or 1950s Cadillac.

ORIENTATION

Bangkok sprawls in an unplanned fashion along the banks of the Mae Nam Chao Phraya, or Chao Phraya River. The railway line heading north from Hualamphong train station neatly divides the central city area into old and new Bangkok.

To the west, the old city is graced with suburbs like leafy Banglamphu, the former royal district of Ratanakosin, with its grand temples and palaces, intense Chinatown (or Yaowarat, as locals call it) and colourful Phahurat, or Little India. Thonburi, the site of the first city settlement and home to Wat Arun, is on the opposite, western bank of the river.

Wat Arun's prang is no accident.

But the distinctions between regions of the new city to the east of Hualamphong are blurred. Locations are more easily defined by roads, rather than suburbs. So you have, for example, the Silom entertainment and business district (around Th Silom and Th Surawong), Sukhumvit (the residential area hugging Th Sukhumvit as it heads east out of the city), the retail hub of Siam Square, the embassy heartland around Th Withayu, as well as the commercial developments and hotels of Th Sathon Tai.

ENVIRONMENT

Your lungs, ears and nose will tell you that Bangkok doesn't have the healthiest of environments. The air quality varies around the city, becoming most stultifying at major intersections, but vehicle emissions are not the only cause of air pollution. Bangkok's air has a relatively high concentration of particulate matter, including dust and debris from construction projects or wheels of cars. The government has tried to maintain 'green lungs' for the city in outlying suburbs, strictly controlling development. Bangkok's also a damned noisy place round the clock, as you'll discover if you stay near a construction site jumping with jackhammers.

There has been an effort to clean up the waterways over recent decades. The results are most noticeable in the river, still used daily by residents for bathing, laundry and drinking water (after treatment). The canals on the Bangkok side are particularly murky – locals cover their faces with handkerchiefs when zipping down them by boat.

You can help Bangkok's environment by drinking out of recyclable glass bottles, using rechargeable batteries and avoiding plastic bags.

GOVERNMENT & POLITICS

Bangkok is the seat of the national government, based on the British constitutional monarchy system but with some subtle differences. The monarch is largely a ceremonial figure (although they appoint high court judges), but is widely worshipped and never publicly criticised. The current monarch, King Bhumibol, is much loved and respected for his public work. Bangkok is in the local government province of Krungthep Mahanaknon (Metropolitan Bangkok), managed by a governor who is appointed by the Ministry of the Interior. Endemic corruption continues to restrict the democratic process at all levels of government, despite plenty of anti-corruption window-dressing by governments.

Thailand is being led by its first CEO-style prime minister, Thaksin Shinawatra, a self-made billionaire who was acquitted of corruption charges in 2001. His Thai Rak Thai Party swept into power in January 2001 with a mandate for sweeping economic reform, but his failure to do this has been frustrating to Thais. The populist Thaksin promised to give every village one million baht for projects to stimulate the domestic economy, though surveys have shown that some villagers are spending the money on consumer goods.

Royal portraits for sale, Th Phra Chan

ECONOMY

Half-finished and abandoned apartment blocks are a constant reminder that Bangkok has not clawed its way out of the doldrums it hit after the 1997 economic meltdown. You'd think that the situation would be better with the country's richest self-made man at the helm, but Thaksin's penchant for populism has meant the economic reform enforced by the International Monetary Fund, as part of its US$17.2 billion rescue package after 1997, has been set aside in the pursuit of a nice set of numbers. The outlook has improved but in the wake of a global economic slowdown some commentators have expressed concerns that Thaksin won't push through the reform necessary for recovery or at least implement it properly.

Bangkok is still the centre of the country's wealth, with the per capita income of your average urbanite well above the national average. During the boom days, every man and his dog seemed to have a property investment on the boil. Industries like banking and finance, tourism, wholesale and retail trade, transport and energy are the biggest revenue earners.

Did You Know?

- Only 10% of Thailand's population, but 60% of its wealth, is based in Bangkok
- Bangkok's minimum daily wage is 162B
- Thailand's GDP is around US$113 billion
- 60% of visitors to Bangkok are male

ARTS
Architecture

In typical Thai style, the functional role of architecture is taken to an artistic level. Traditional Bangkok houses were built over the river or canals on stilts, either single-room houses or houses interconnected by walkways, but always built in teak. Rooflines were steep and often decorated with spiritual motifs.

Traditionally, temples have several core components: a *bòt*, a *wíhāan* and a *chedi*. Influences of different cultures and eras in Thai history are seen

most vividly in temple architecture. Most Bangkok temples are in Ratanakosin, or Bangkok, style, which is relatively simple.

European influence became more apparent near the end of the 19th century, first with classic Ratanakosin buildings like Vimanmek Teak Mansion, then followed by Thai Deco, with examples like Hualamphong train station. During the property boom of the 1980s, Thai architects let their hair down – the Bank of Asia building, aka the Robot Building, is a classic reminder.

Wat Pho's temple roof reaches for the sky.

Music

Little-heard outside the country, classical Thai music can sound unusual to the Western ear, but quite entrancing. The classical orchestra, called the *pìiphâat*, was developed to accompany classical dance-dramas but now you'll probably only hear it at a temple fair or performance. It has anything from five to 20 players who perform on traditional Thai instruments such as the *phin*, whose strings are plucked by musicians, the *kháwng wong yài*, an extraordinary piece with tuned drums arranged in a circular shape, and the *tà-phon* drum.

Modern Thai music is not so unique. Taxi drivers love listening to *lûuk thûng*, Thai country music from the northeastern provinces. It has a defi-

Renegade Sculptor

A Bangkok temple sculptor has taken his art form into the new millennium. While working at Wat Poriwat on the southeastern outskirts of Bangkok, he carved an enormous David Beckham, standing it amid sacred Buddha images. And on another unnamed temple, he carved the profile of Osama bin Laden into some wooden detail.

nite croon feel to it, though the subject matter mines faithful country and western themes of losing your job, your wife and your buffalo. Jazz blends Western styles with traditional melodies and rhythms and is much more sophisticated than the music coming from cutesy-poo local pop stars, who are hugely popular.

Theatre & Dance

Of the six traditional dramatic forms, you're most likely to come into contact with *khon*. It's expensive, extravagant and a visual feast, where hundreds of masked monkeys, demons, men and women love and die, fight and dance.

Acted only by men, khon drama is based upon stories of the *Ramayana* and was traditionally only for royal audiences. It was in danger of dying out for many years but is slowly being revived and is performed at a few venues around Bangkok.

Only women traditionally performed and sang for lower nobility in *lákhon nai*, which takes elements of the *Ramayana* and traditional folk tales. Closely related, *lákhon nâwk* focuses on folk tales and may have men or women actors. A variation, called *lákhon kâe bon*, is played out at shrines like Lak Meuang – the musicians and dancers are hired by worshippers to earn merit. Yet another *lákhon* form is the most like Western theatre – in *lákhon phûut* the players speak, instead of sing.

> ### Ol' Blue Eyes
> The biggest *lûuk thûng* star is a smiling Norwegian lad with a prominent cowlick by the name of Jonas Anderson. With his singing and dancing partner, Christy Gibson, he's mobbed by fans, stars on TV and meets royalty. Everyone loves the blond-haired singer's perfect Thai intonation, picked up from years living in northeastern Thailand, as he sings the songs of lovelorn farmers.

Like many South-East Asian countries, Thailand has a great tradition of shadow-puppet theatre, where 'flat' puppets are moved behind a lit cloth screen. But performances in Bangkok these days are rare. Royalty enjoyed *lákhon lék* performances by marionettes. The National Museum has some well-preserved marionettes from the time of Rama V, when they were rather fashionable.

Visual Arts

Thailand's artistic traditions date back thousands of years – Bangkok museums have many examples of the prehistoric Ban Chiang pottery. But the most captivating of traditional art are sculpted Buddha images, carved and moulded out of jade, ivory, metal, stone, marble or wood. Painting was limited to intricate representations of the stories of the *Ramakian*, Thailand's version of India's epic *Ramayana*, and *jataka*, tales of the Buddha's past lives.

Thai art didn't move beyond the religious until well into the 20th century and Bangkok artists, along with their Chiang Mai contemporaries, have driven the modern art scene. Italian artist Corrado Feroci was incredibly influential – he designed Democracy Monument and developed the first fine arts department, now at Silpakorn University.

Murals depicting scenes from the Ramakian, Wat Phra Kaew.

SOCIETY & CULTURE

Surrounded by advertising billboards shouting Western brands and neon-lit multinational chains, you might feel that Bangkok has willingly surrendered to Western culture. But behind the scenes a Thai value system is ticking away, guiding every aspect of life. When a local falls about laughing when you trip over spectacularly, they're trying to save face on your behalf, not indulge in *Schadenfreude*. Westerners used to rapid-fire service may get frustrated with bank workers cracking jokes with each other instead of serving immediately – but this is just sànùk (fun) in action. Sànùk means making everything, even the most menial task, fun. When Thais get charged less to enter the museum than you, it's not because they don't like foreign-

ers – they just think you are of higher status financially, so you should look after Thais by paying more. Status – whether it be financial, age-related or your level of power – governs every relationship.

Almost all Thais are Theravada Buddhists. Thai Buddhists aim to be reborn into a better life by making merit, which can mean making donations to temples or feeding monks. Every Thai male is expected to become a monk for a short time.

Etiquette

Just remember to respect two things: religion and the monarchy. This means standing still when the national anthem is played, before every movie and at 8am and 6pm daily; not criticising the king or his family; and dressing respectfully at royal buildings and temples (with shoulders and legs covered, and shoes removed before entering a building with a sacred Buddha image). Keep your feet pointed away from a Buddha image. Monks aren't supposed to touch or be touched by women.

Other ways to avoid offending Thais include: not wearing shoes inside people's homes; dressing modestly, not like you're on the beach; not touching anyone's head; not pointing your feet at people, nor touching them with your foot; and not passing things to people with your left hand.

Remember to keep your cool – getting angry or talking loudly is thought rude – and speak softly and smile a lot. Losing your temper is considered a major loss of face for both parties.

When to Wâi

The traditional Thai greeting is the **wâi**, a gesture where palms are put together, prayer-like. The amount of bowing that accompanies a wâi is a delicate formula, dependent on the status of the two people wâi-ing each other. But you're best to take the attitude: if someone wâis you, wâi them back, unless they're a child or someone serving you, like a waiter.

highlights

Bangkok's history of haphazard planning means you'll have the best experiences in the most unlikely of places. Just when you start despairing at the predominance of concrete and cars, a wafting scent of incense leads you to a serene temple in an area you'd written off as soulless.

The heat and humidity can make the hardiest sightseer wilt, while the sheer logistics and hassles of getting around in 'The City Where Anything Goes But The Traffic' can be incredibly frustrating. You need a plan of attack – pinpoint an area and head there via a traffic-resistant medium (ie, Skytrain or Chao Phraya River Express boat or taxi in off-peak times). Don't try to do it all in a few days – you can't, anyway, and you'll miss the subtleties that make this city so intriguing.

Lowlights

Bangkok can take you so, so high – and then so, so low, when there's:

- traffic gridlock and pollution
- oppressive heat and humidity
- dodgy taxi-drivers and touts

Stopping Over

One Day Visit the Grand Palace and Wat Phra Kaew, then soothe your feet with a traditional Thai massage at Wat Pho. Catch a river express boat to Chinatown and explore the markets and alleyways.

Two Days Wander around Lumphini Park in the morning. Catch the Skytrain to Chatuchak Weekend Market. Get architectural at Jim Thompson's House. Bar-hop your way up Soi 4 in Silom.

Three Days Explore the Dusit's palaces and museums. Climb the Golden Mount at Wat Saket for the views. Have lunch at a riverside restaurant. Take the river express boat to Nonthaburi or indulge in retail therapy around Siam Square or Th Sukhumvit. At night, catch a *muay thai* match or linger over an authentic Thai meal.

Stupefying chedi panorama at Wat Pho

ABHISEK DUSIT THRONE HALL   (2, A9)

This East-meets-West royal building is classic Chulalongkorn. Officially known as Rama V, King Chulalongkorn took much inspiration from his European tutors and was the first Thai monarch to visit the continent. Visions of Moorish palaces and Victorian mansions must have still been spinning around in his head when he commissioned the throne hall (completed 1904) as it is a stunning, intricate building which, despite all its porticoes and other Western influences, has a distinctly Thai exterior. Built as the throne hall for the palace (they are separated by a canal), it opens onto a big stretch of lawn and flowerbeds, just like any important European building. As with all Thai royal buildings, visitors should dress appropriately.

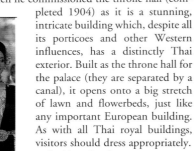

INFORMATION

- ✉ Dusit Park, Th Ratchawithi, Dusit
- ☎ 02 628 6300
- 🚌 air-con 10, 16, 18
- ⚓ Thewet
- ⏲ 9.30am-4pm
- 💲 50/20B (free with Grand Palace ticket)
- ♿ limited
- ✕ park restaurant

Inside, the heavy ornamentation of the white main room is quite extraordinary, especially if you've been visiting at a lot of overwhelmingly gold temples or wooden traditional buildings. Look up to just below the roofline to view the line of brightly coloured, **stained-glass panels** in Moorish patterns.

The authentic collection of regional handicraft kept inside the building is proudly Thai. The exhibits are made by members of the Support foundation, sponsored by Queen Sirikit to keep traditional skills alive. You'll probably not see anything like the quality of the *málaeng tháp* **collages**, where dead metallic beetles' wings decorate silverware or wood carvings, anywhere else. Other sections worth hunting out include the **textiles**, with striking examples of traditional styles of the different regions, and **bamboo basketry** in north-eastern designs.

Western influences are evident in King Chulalongkorn's Abhisek Dusit Throne Hall.

DON'T MISS
- bamboo basketry • *málaeng tháp* collages • traditional textiles
- Moorish-style stained-glass panels along the roofline
- a stroll under the porticoes

CHATUCHAK WEEKEND MARKET (5)

Chatuchak is no ordinary flea market, where you casually pick through a few stalls of second-hand books, jewellery and clothes. Think of a minimum of 7000 stalls selling goods like fighting cocks, buffalo horns and opium pipes. Then picture hundreds of thousands of visitors a day, crowding and bargaining and browsing.

And then imagine all this on an even bigger scale and open every day, which will become a reality in a year or so when a new section is finished.

Overwhelming? You bet – but there's no more fascinating shopping experience in Bangkok. Before the Skytrain days, it used to take over an hour to trek out to Chatuchak by bus; now the new trains whizz you there in 15mins. Take a copy of *Nancy Chandler's Map of Bangkok*, which has informative annotations, so you can start with the good intention of focusing on the areas you really want to see (though you'll inevitably get lost and find the buy of the century). You really can't see it all in one day, even if you have superhuman powers of resisting heat (there's no air-conditioning) and claustrophobia.

In theory, Chatuchak is organised into logical sections like **antiques**, **wildlife**, **flowers**, **clothing**, **plants** and **crafts**, but this delineation has deteriorated somewhat over the years. Clothes shops seem to dominate – many young designers start out with stalls here – and you can find good everyday Thai pieces, like sarongs for men and women, farmers' pants and shirts, and second-hand jeans and shirts.

INFORMATION

- ✉ Chatuchak Park, Th Phahonyothin, Chatuchak
- 🚇 Mo Chit
- 🚌 air-con 2, 3, 9, 10, 12, 13
- ⏱ Sat-Sun 8am-6pm
- 💲 free
- ℹ TAT office (☎ 02 272 4448)
- ✗ Viva's

Chatuchak Market mayhem

Wildlife for Sale

The animal section is one of the most fun sections of Chatuchak Weekend Market – hyperactive tropical fish, cute puppies, slithering snakes. But it's also a trading ground for wildlife, like Australian parrots, smuggled out illegally from other countries.

CHINATOWN (2, J6)

Quite simply, Chinatown is the most fascinating district in Bangkok. It's noisy and smelly and exhilarating. It's an area of dark laneways and traffic-choked arterial roads, of bright, cheap markets and enticing foodstalls as far as the eye can see. You know you're in Chinatown when the shops sell just one line of goods, whether it be rubber bathplugs, plastic bags or coffins.

INFORMATION
- Tha Ratchawong
- White Orchid (p. 79)

Enjoying a meal, Chinatown.

This business philosophy sometimes extends to entire alleyways – like the infamous arms-dealers' strips.

It's tough to define, but Chinatown could be approximately described as the area west of Hualamphong train station and east of Khlong Ong Ang, between Th Charoen Krung and the river. A Chinese population was moved there to make way for the new capital at Ratanakosin. In the late 19th century it became notorious for its underworld – an 1882 census recorded 245 opium dens, 154 pawnshops, 69 gambling establishments and 26 brothels. **Sampeng Lane** was in the thick of the seedy action, as the famous **Nakhon Kasem (Thieves Market)** was a channel for stolen goods. In the 1920s and 30s, stunning Thai Art Deco buildings were built along Chinatown's main streets, **Th Yaowarat** (now known for its gold shops) and **Th Charoen Krung**. Today, Chinatown is still the undisputed Chinese centre of Bangkok, boasting four Chinese-language newspapers and an amazing Chinese new year festival.

Catch the river express boat to Chinatown and just wander. You won't know what we're on about until you get lost down a laneway, lined with traditional wooden shophouses, with an extended family and business under the same roof.

Vegetarian Festival

For the first nine days of the ninth lunar month (around September-October), Chinatown celebrates its annual Vegetarian Festival. The festivities are centred on Wat Mangkon Kamalawat (2, K8), however, restaurants and street stalls in the area get into the spirit by whipping up some amazing vegetarian Thai and Chinese dishes.

JIM THOMPSON'S HOUSE (3, B6)

If the art and architecture of Jim Thompson's House doesn't grip you, its former owner will. American-born Thompson was an intriguing chap both in life and death – he disappeared without trace during an afternoon stroll in Malaysia's Cameron Highlands in 1967. His legacy is a Thai silk industry revered the world over, a divine collection of **South-East Asian art**, a serene assembly of **traditional Thai homes** and a raft of conspiracy theories (but more on that later).

The tour guide will take you through some of the six teak houses on stilts that he brought to the site beside Khlong Saen Saep in 1959 (he didn't move in until a day astrologers deemed suitably auspicious). Some of the houses are centuries old; all are built without nails and with the traditional sloping wall, door and window design. Thompson, who had served in Thailand during WWII, brought his great passion for art to Bangkok after the war, finding New York a tad quiet. His art collection and personal possessions – including rare Chinese porcelain pieces, like a mouse house, as well as Burmese, Cambodian and Thai artefacts – are displayed throughout the site, overgrown with lush tropical gardens punctuated by lotus ponds. You can also poke through his

INFORMATION

✉ Soi Kasem San 2, Th Phra Ram I, Siam Sq
☎ 02 215 0122
🚇 National Stadium
🚌 air-con 8
⛴ canal taxi to Ratchathewi
🕐 9am-4.30pm
💲 100/50B adults/ children & students
ℹ compulsory tours (English & French) every 10mins
🍴 Jim Thompson Cafe

His house is here, but where's Jim?

What *Was* that Bump in the Road?

Conspiracies abound on the fate of Bangkok's most famous expat. Some muse that he was snatched by communist spies, while others say he met his maker between the fangs of a man-eating tiger. Much less fascinating, but far more likely, is that he was run over by a Malaysian truck driver.

library, the only room with glassed-in windows (he weakened and installed air-conditioning).

But undoubtedly Thompson's keen eye for design was best used to revive a Thai cottage industry under the threat of extinction. He sent samples of hand-woven silk to European fashion houses, creating a demand for traditional skills that continues to this day.

GRAND PALACE & WAT PHRA KAEW (2, H3)

The Grand Palace and Wat Phra Kaew are the Big Kahunas of the Bangkok tourist trail. But these heavyweights deserve every bit of attention lavished upon them (except from the mercurial touts outside who spring at you from all directions). They are, indeed, grand, artistically superb and steeped in significance.

INFORMATION

- ✉ Th Na Phra Lan, Ratanakosin
- ☎ 02 224 1833
- 🌐 www.palaces.thai.net
- 🚌 air-con 3, 6, 8, 12, 44
- ⚓ Tha Chang
- ⏱ 8.30am-3.30pm
- 💲 200B (includes entry to Dusit museums, including Vimanmek Teak Mansion)
- ℹ English tours 10am, 10.30am, 1.30pm & 2pm
- ♿ good
- ✕ Krisa Coffee Shop

Statue at the compound entrance of the Royal Monastery of the Emerald Buddha, Wat Phra Kaew

Wat Phra Kaew (Temple of the Emerald Buddha) is the holiest temple in the country, housing its most sacred Buddha image. But it can be hard to see the diminutive Buddha image (carved of nephrite) on its pedestal for all the incredible surrounding ornamentation. It will be wearing one of three royal robes (Rama I arranged for it to have appropriate apparel for the hot and rainy seasons, then Rama III gave it another cool-season outfit). The king changes the robes in a serious ceremony three times a year.

Wat Phra Kaew adjoins the palace on vast grounds consecrated when Rama I moved the capital to Bangkok in 1782. Successive kings and their families lived in the palace compound until Rama V moved the royal seat to Dusit – today the Grand Palace is mostly used only for ceremonies, like Coronation Day. Previous kings used to house their substantial harems in **Chakri Mahaprasat (Grand Palace Hall),** built in 1882 by a British architect, who instilled it with Renaissance and Thai-style features. **Amarindra Hall**, a former hall of justice, is now used for coronations.

Even if you've got traditional architecture fatigue, just wandering around the 100 or so buildings (spread over 945,000 sq metres), most of them classic Ratanakosin architecture, is a highlight. Each building is designed with such incredible detail – lined with mosaic, some surrounded by many intricate figures. You'll need to wear sunglasses just to deal with the shards of light bouncing off golden detail on buildings, polished to within an inch of their life, let alone the magnificent golden chedi.

The Emerald Buddha

The Emerald Buddha may only be 66cm tall, but it is heavy with the weight of spiritual significance as Thailand's most important image.

Its history is hazy, involving travels across the Indian subcontinent, Laos and Thailand. With Rama I's help, it first called Bangkok home over 200 years ago.

To escape the heat, retreat to the shady cloisters, lined with Rama I-era murals which tell the entire *Ramakian* story. To see the story from start to finish, work your way around clockwise from the northern gate.

Because this complex is so sacred, you must be dressed appropriately – you should wear covered shoes, and also cover your legs (Thai farmers' pants are not acceptable) and shoulders. If you don't mind wearing clothes that have done many stinky trips around the complex, you can borrow proper attire from the main office. Remove your shoes before entering the main chapel of Wat Phra Kaew.

Left: The colourful structures of Wat Phra Kaew
Right: Wall Painting, Wat Phra Kaew

LETTUCE FARM PALACE   (1, G3)

A wander around the peaceful gardens of Lettuce Farm Palace, or Wang Suan Phakkat, and inside its traditional buildings, especially the magnificent Lacquer Pavilion, can make you feel a million miles from central Bangkok. The palace grounds were once a cabbage patch and later the site of the home of Princess Chumbon of Nakhon Sawan, the architect behind the gardens (but not born in the cabbage patch, as far as we know). But now the palace's six houses, connected by covered wooden walkways and full of art, antiques and ancient artefacts, are permanently open to the public.

INFORMATION

- ⊠ Th Sri Ayuthaya, Ratchathewi
- ☎ 02 245 4934
- 🚊 Phayathai
- 🚌 air-con 13, 18, 38, 139, 140
- ◷ 9am-4pm
- ⑤ 100B
- ⓘ information centre below House IV

The complex's most famous exhibit, the **Lacquer Pavilion**, sits on stilts at the back of the property. Taken from a monastery near Ayuthaya, the tiny building has an exterior lined with wood carvings and interior decorated with intricate gold-leaf and black-lacquer *jataka* (stories of the Buddha) and *Ramayana* murals. Just nearby, a **royal barge** is stored on one of the many little canals that run through the property.

You'll uncover a mix of stuff in the rest of the buildings. If you're interested in khon performance, head for the small museum just near House VI which shows how the elaborate masks are created. House II has a curious collection of ceremonial **fans**, while House I boasts a magnificent **U-Thong seated Buddha image**. Prehistory buffs will have a field day with the exhibits of House V and VI. The princess appears to have been quite the shell and mineral enthusiast, as you'll see in her collections.

Dancers masks at the Khon museum at Lettuce Farm Palace

DON'T MISS
- Lacquer Pavilion • Khon museum • ceremonial fans
- U-Thong Buddha image • a walk around the gardens

LUMPHINI PARK (3, F10)

A morning visit to Bangkok's biggest green lung is a must-do. Try to get there around 7am, when all the action starts. The pathways are crammed with people gliding into tai chi poses or kicking up their heels at dancing classes. Groups of old folk settle under trees for what looks like an open-air karaoke session, minus the TV screen (the warbled songs are most definitely an acquired taste). Buff beefcakes colonise the weights corner with an air of intimidation. The vendors carefully arrange their stalls of snake blood and bile, popular health tonics for Chinese and Thais, for the day's business. Chess players settle in for a duel to the death, while joggers pound their way around the park. And then it all stops, suddenly, when the royal anthem is played at 8am.

Lumphini Park is named after the Buddha's birthplace in Nepal and can be entered via any of the gates on Th Phra Ram IV, Th Sarasin, Th Ratchadamri and Th Withayu.

As you've probably realised, it's the best free entertainment in town, even more so during the concerts put on by the Bangkok Light Symphony Orchestra in the cool months or during kite-flying season, when there are colourful kite stalls and dashing antics in the skies above. If you are prepared to spend a few baht, you can hire one

INFORMATION

- ✉ Th Phra Ram IV, btw Th Withayu & Th Ratchadamri
- 🚇 Sala Daeng
- 🚌 air-con 7, 15, 67, 141
- 🕐 5am-8pm
- 💲 free
- ℹ free concerts Nov/Dec-Feb around 5pm, call the Bangkok Tourist Bureau for more info; tourist police office (☎ 1155)
- ♿ excellent
- ✖ food stalls on northern boundary

Go fly a kite in Lumphini Park.

Nice Doggy?

Be careful of dogs in Lumphini Park – there have been several reports of people being bitten by rabid dogs. A bite, lick or scratch from an infected animal should be cleaned immediately, then you should seek medical help.

of the paddleboats that putter around the enormous ornamental lake. But you don't need to part with any money in order to experience the feeling that you've escaped from the big smoke, if only for a moment.

NATIONAL MUSEUM   (6, E1)

If the National Museum was a person, it would be a scatterbrained yet brilliant university lecturer. Why? Its collections are top-rate but don't follow a strict train of thought, meaning you don't get a stern-faced chronological tour through Thai history since the year dot. South-East Asia's biggest

museum is made up of many separate buildings – originally built in 1782 as a palace but turned into a museum by Rama V in 1884 – spread across a large block just over the road from Sanam Luang.

Poke your nose into Room 17 to gawk at the enormous, elaborate **funeral chariots** which carried the ashes of royalty; the ones here were used by lesser royals, like Rama I's big sister. You can get a few insights into migration from the **musical instruments** in Room 15, which displays the instruments of a Phat Mon ensemble, a popular form of music introduced by the Mon people (whose descendants live on Ko Kret) from Burma. The money collection – including fat Sukhothai coins said to have magical properties and the long 'Hoi' money used in the north – is surprisingly fascinating. If you're even remotely interested in art, you should take the time to see the sections in the main southern and northern buildings – the guided tours will help you to understand the most important pieces. Before you leave, visit the restored **Buddhaisawan (Phutthaisawan) Chapel** to see one of Thailand's most revered Buddha images, Phra Phuttha Sihing, and the golden teak **Tamnak Daeng** house nearby.

A landscaped courtyard surrounds South-East Asia's biggest museum.

DON'T MISS
• traditional musical instruments • Buddhaisawan (Phutthaisawan) Chapel & Phra Phuttha Sihing • funeral chariots • art & archaeology collections • Tamnak Daeng pavilion

NONTHABURI BY BOAT   (1, D1)

There's nothing like a leisurely boat trip to soothe the soul. And the journey up the mighty Mae Nam Chao Phraya on a river express boat will show you a side of Bangkok you'll never

see in the back seat of a taxi. The trip to Nonthaburi can take anything from 50-90mins, depending on whether you catch a special express boat or one that makes every stop.

If you want to get the most out of your 12B fare or just make sure you get a seat, start at Tha Ratchasingkhon (1, J1). As you head upriver, you'll notice key landmarks of the old farang quarter on your right, like the **Oriental Hotel's Authors Wing** (3, J2) and crumbling **Customs House** (3, H2).

After a while, striking **Wat Arun** (2, K2) looms on your left and then the ornate **Grand Palace and Wat Phra Kaew** (2, G3) on your right. Not far away is the mouth of **Khlong Bangkok Noi** (2, E2), an alternate waterway route to Nonthaburi, on the left. Once you leave the city centre behind, the landscape becomes dominated by palm trees, lush greenery, houses and temple complexes. The daily cycle of life on the river carries on around you, as locals wash and fish, and coalhulks lumber past.

Longtail boat drivers wait for passengers, Nonthaburi pier.

Durians

Nonthaburi is proud of its durians. Replicas of the spikey things, considered the king of fruit by many Thais, decorate its riverside promenade, but luckily these durians are made of metal and don't exude the pungent aroma that many Thai hotels and Thai International Airways have banned from their premises.

Nonthaburi arrives almost all too quickly. If you need a snack before returning to Bangkok, use your new-found sea legs at the floating restaurant to the right as you step off the jetty.

ROYAL BARGES NATIONAL MUSEUM (2, D1)

The tradition of Thai royalty travelling by ornate and often outlandish barges stems back to the glory days of Ayuthaya. When Bangkok became the capital, the spectacle continued – an incredible sight of hundreds of men rowing, chanting or holding colourful umbrellas over the royals as the golden boats glided down the waterways and glinted in the sunlight.

INFORMATION

- ✉ Khlong Bangkok Noi, Thonburi
- ☎ 02 424 0004
- 🚌 3, 81
- 🚉 Tha Rot Fai or take a longtail
- 🕐 9am-5pm (except 31 Dec, 1 Jan, 12-14 Apr)
- 💲 30B (100B if you want to take photos)
- ♿ good

These days, the royals rarely take to the water, which is understandable when you consider the effort involved.

For the king to head out in his personal barge, the glorious *Supphannahong* (golden swan), he needs the help of 50 crew, seven umbrella bearers, two helmsmen, two navigators, a flagman, a rhythm-keeper and a chanter. *Supphannahong*, which now lives at the Royal Barges National Museum, is 50m long and made out of a single piece of timber, making it the world's largest dugout boat.

Many of the museum's barges were once used in the royal navy but are now fragile (some were bombed in WWII but have since been restored) and saved for royal ceremonies.

The newest one is *Narai Song Suban*, which was built to commemorate the king's 50th anniversary. The ritual of the barge procession, explained in photographic and multimedia displays, is quite intriguing.

It's far better to take a longtail boat to the museum. Note that if you walk in via the curving walkway, you might be hassled by touts in collusion with museum staff.

Take a Bow

The dramatic figureheads on the bows of royal barges are usually based upon creatures of Hindu mythology, such as the *garuda* (eagle-man), monkey or sea animals like a crocodile and a fish.

SANAM LUANG (6, E2)

Lumphini Park may be the green heart of Bangkok but Sanam Luang (Royal Field) is its ceremonial soul. This Ratanakosin park, just north of the Grand Palace, is where royals are cremated (including many from the Chakri dynasty) and the annual May **ploughing ceremony** that kicks off the rice-growing season is held. But it's not just the official-dom it presides over that makes this park so spiritually important to the city. It's where the locals meet and hold protests, where the weekend flea market was held before it moved to Chatuchak, where **kite**

Kite Fights

During kite-fighting season, between February and April, the skies above Sanam Luang become a dangerous, hotly contested territory. Fights are held between many teams, who fly either a 'male' or 'female' kite and are assigned a particular territory, winning points if they can force a competitor into their zone.

Kite-fighting's version of Mike Tyson?

enthusiasts have taken to the skies since the 19th century and where **amulet sellers** gather. Locals have been outraged at the local government's plans to fence off and shut down their park at night in order to keep prostitutes and the homeless people out.

If you are in Bangkok in May, try to experience the Royal Ploughing Ceremony. The king usually presides over the 2hr event, held just before the rains arrive, while the agriculture minister assumes the role of Lord of the Ploughing, dressed in a conical hat and glittering robes. He follows two white oxen as they pull a plough through consecrated areas and then sow seeds, the year's first planting. But it's the fickle tastes of oxen (they are presented with seven buckets of different feeds) that predict the nation's agricultural production, domestic transport and foreign affairs for the year.

A statue of the earth goddess Mae Thorani stands in a pavilion at the park's northern end – it was originally attached to a well that locals drank from.

VIMANMEK TEAK MANSION (2, A8)

This enormous golden-teak mansion began its life on Ko Si Chang, in the Gulf of Thailand, in 1868. But then in the early 20th century Rama V, or Chulalongkorn, needed somewhere to house his wife, children and concubines, so he had it dismantled and reassembled, reputedly without nails, on his new palace complex in Dusit. The king took a three-storey octagonal apartment for himself and decorated his new home with more than a passing reference to the grand Victorian palaces he had seen in Europe. Women lived in a special green-coloured wing (the only men allowed inside were Chulalongkorn, a monk, a doctor and small boys) and a giant mirror on the main staircase was installed as a security device.

INFORMATION

- ✉ Th Ratwithi, Dusit
- ☎ 02 628 6300
- 🚌 air-con 10, 16,18
- ⚓ Tha Thewet
- ◷ 9.30am-3.15pm
- 💲 50/20B
- ⓘ hr-long tours every half-hr 9.30am-3pm, Thai classical & folk dances 10.30am & 2pm in pavilion on canal side.
- ♿ limited
- ✖ park restaurant

Its 81 rooms are elegant and overwhelmingly pastel, with walls painted either beige, blue, green, ivory or pink. But the highlight, besides the architecture, is checking out Chulalongkorn's personal effects and antiques – including **grand pianos**, beautiful **Ching dynasty pieces** and the **first menu in Thailand** – and getting an insight into how the royals lived. The staff won't let you in on a compulsory free tour if you aren't dressed properly (ie, legs and shoulders covered).

Until it was reopened in 1982, the mansion hadn't been used since 1932. A mark in the floorboards is the only reminder of its WWII bombing. Thais believe an important Buddha image protected the building from great damage during the bomb attack, which hit just near the room storing the image.

Stunning Vimanmek Teak Mansion

DON'T MISS
- traditional dance performances ● grand staircases
- Chulalongkorn's antiques & personal possessions

WAT ARUN (2, K2)

As you chug along the Chao Phraya by boat, the simplicity and pure lines of Wat Arun on the Thonburi bank never cease to captivate you. Hold that image in your mind because it's the best one you'll get of the Temple of Dawn. The up-close-and-personal reality is nothing as romantic – to even look at the *prang* (tower) you have to step around traditionally dressed dancers droning into their mobile phones and aggressive stall-holders. It's quite unsettling to see this sacred site – the last home of the Emerald Buddha before Rama I brought it across the river – become such a hub of trashy tourism. The wat was built on the site of the former palace and royal temple of King Taksin.

But persevere and you'll be trying desperately to resist not touching the rugged exterior of the **prang**, rising 82m into the air, covered with plaster and embedded with a mosaic of colourful patterned Chinese porcelain and seashells. This decoration was quite common in the early Ratanakosin period, when Chinese ships calling at Bangkok would use tonnes of porcelain as ballast. Climb the steep stairs up the prang, built in the first half of the 19th century, for views of the city. The prang's design is considered unique in the way it combines Khmer and Thai influences.

You might find some peace at the **bòt** , where the main Buddha image is said to have been designed by Rama II, and on your way back to the ferry, stop at the **sacred banyan tree**.

INFORMATION

✉ Th Arun Amarin, Bangkok Yai
☎ 02 466 3167
🚍 19, 57, 83
⛴ cross-river ferry from Tha Tien
🕐 9am-5pm
💲 20B

The towering Wat Arun prang

DON'T MISS
- climbing up the prang ● porcelain-embedded prang exterior
- main Buddha image at the bòt ● bòt murals
- sacred banyan tree

WAT MAHATHAT (2, F3)

The rambling Wat Mahathat compound in Ratanakosin is the most important centre of Buddhist learning in South-East Asia. Its **Buddhist university**, Mahathat Rajavidyalaya, attracts monks from Laos, Cambodia and Vietnam, while its wat is the national centre of the Mahanikai monastic sect.

The Mahanikai sect is one of the two sects that make up the Sangha, or Buddhist brotherhood, in Thailand. Members of both sects must adhere to the 227 monastic vows laid out in the Buddhist scriptures, but there are subtle differences between the two. For example, Mahanikais eat twice before noon and may accept side dishes, while Thammayut monks must be more disciplined by eating only once a day, before noon, and only eating what is in their alms bowl.

Wat Mahathat was built in the Ayuthaya period, but has changed its appearance (through renovation) and name many times. Over the years, it has evolved into an informal community centre and is always bustling with visitors and monks. You'll probably feel more comfortable here than at any other temple in Bangkok, making it well

INFORMATION

- ✉ 3 Th Maharaj, Ratanakosin
- ☎ 02 221 5999
- 🚌 air-con 3, 6
- ⚓ Tha Maharat
- 🕐 9am-5pm
- 💲 free
- ♿ limited

Lotus flower offering, Wat Mahathat

worth a visit if you're particularly curious about the day-to-day workings of Buddhism. The monastery is also a renowned **meditation** centre (p. 44).

A daily **open-air market** sells Thai herbal medicine remedies, while on weekends stall-holders set up a produce market on the temple grounds. Just opposite the main entrance, on the other side of Th Mahathat, is a well-known **amulet market** – the locals call it *talát phrá khrêuang*, or holy amulet market.

Traditional Thai Medicine

The area around Wat Mahathat is renowned for traditional herbal medicine shops. Traditional Thai medical theory is similar to both Ayurvedic and Chinese medicine traditions, and takes a holistic approach to health. Healers may prescribe treatment through massage, herbal medicine or psycho-spiritual healing. Medicines are created from among 700 plant varieties.

WAT PHO   (2, J3)

Wat Pho is a heavyweight on the Bangkok temple scene. With a birthday dating from the 16th century, it's even older than Bangkok itself; it can also lay claim to being the biggest temple. Still not impressed? It has the nation's largest collection of Buddha images, including an incredible reclining Buddha image which just happens to be Thailand's longest.

INFORMATION

✉ Th Chetuphon, Ratanakosin
☎ 02 222 0094
🚌 air-con 1, 7, 8
⛴ Tha Tien
🕐 8am-5pm
💲 20B
♿ good

Superlatives aside, Wat Pho is just an interesting place to wander around. Its grounds are divided by Th Chetuphon and each section is surrounded by thick whitewashed walls. Though it came into existence over 400 years ago, this temple's history really begins in 1781, when the original monastery was completely rebuilt.

The northern compound is extensive, but many visitors home in on the *wíhãan* housing the **45m-long reclining Buddha image** with the amazing feet. Its big, beautiful soles are inlaid with mother-of-pearl to create 108 auspicious *laksana*, or characteristics of the Buddha. Once you're away from this wíhãan, you can explore the compound at will without tourist groups cramping your style. Look for the big **bòt** surrounded by a gallery of Buddha images and four wíhãan, **large chedis** commemorating the first three Chakri kings, plus 91 smaller chedis, and a school building where classes in Buddhist philosophy are held.

Most people know Wat Pho as the national nerve centre, so to speak, of traditional Thai massage. So if your feet are weary, head to the eastern edge of the complex, where the famous **traditional massage centre** is based (p. 45).

Left to right: Feet of the reclining Buddha; monks at morning prayers; chedi detail

DON'T MISS
- a massage ● the reclining Buddha image's feet
- the northern compound's bòt surrounded by Buddha images
- chedis commemorating the Chakri kings

WAT SAKET & GOLDEN MOUNT   (2, G7)

From the top of Wat Saket's Golden Mount you have clear **views of the city rooftops**, though it might not be quite so idyllic as American writer Frank Vincent's outlook in 1871. Vincent wrote in *The Land of the White Elephant* that 'the general appearance of Bangkok is that of a large primitive village, situated in and mostly concealed by a virgin forest of almost impenetrable density'. Nevertheless, the long, steady walk up tiny stairs around the mount is quite scenic, with walls heavy with vines and lines of temple bells at intervals along the way. During the temple festival in November, a beautiful candlelit procession winds its way around to the top.

The hill itself is artificial, built when a big chedi commissioned by Rama III collapsed due to its soft soil base. After being left to ruin, Rama IV built a small chedi on its crest and, later, Rama V added to it and stored an Indian Buddha relic in the chedi. It wasn't until during WWII that the hill was finally secure, after being reinforced with concrete walls. You don't need to pay to climb the hill, but you will be expected to make a 10B donation to ascend the steep stairs to the lookout.

As for Wat Saket, built during the time of Rama I, it is fairly unimpressive and not really worth your time. The monastery library was originally built over water, but the pond was later cemented over.

Top: A row of Buddhas around the Consecration Hall, Wat Saket
Bottom: View from the Golden Mount

Temple Talk

Not quite sure whether it's a chedi, bòt or stupa? A bòt is a consecrated hall for ordinations of monks and looks like a wíhāan, which stores important Buddha images but is bigger than a bòt. Chedis, also known as stupa, are distinctive monuments which often contain fragments of the Buddha or a king's ashes.

WAT TRAIMIT (2, L9)

You only visit Wat Traimit for one reason, one very big reason – **the world's largest golden Buddha image** which weighs a whopping 5.5 tonnes and stands 3m tall. If it wasn't for an opportune accident, this Sukhothai-era image could still be undiscovered.

A plaster-coated Buddha image had been stored in a temporary shelter. Then, in 1955, workers began to move it to more permanent digs in the current temple when it fell from the crane, cracking the coating. Rain further weakened it and later workers were astonished to discover a bewitching golden gleam beneath. Apparently it was quite common to cover valuable Buddha images during the late Sukhothai and early Ayuthaya periods, when the threat of Burmese invaders was very real (indeed, they brought down the Ayuthaya era). Now, almost 50 years down the track,

INFORMATION

- ✉ Th Traimit, Chinatown
- ☎ 02 623 1226
- 🚆 regional train to Hualamphong
- 🚌 53
- ⏱ 8am-5pm
- 💲 20B
- ♿ limited
- 🍴 About Studio/About Cafe (p. 92)

Sukhothai

The art from the Sukhothai era (mid-13th to late-14th century), when Wat Traimit's famous Buddha image was created, is considered to be the most classical of all styles. During this time, Buddha images became more elongated and slimmer, and for the first time were portrayed walking.

the Buddha is beautifully polished and Wat Traimit, or Temple of the Golden Buddha, is a must-see on the tourist trail.

A short distance west of Hualamphong train station, the wat housing this solid-gold image is nothing special but dates from the 13th century. The complex is usually crowded with snap-happy tourists, locals making merit by rubbing gold leaf on smaller Buddha images and, most curiously at a place of worship, money changers. Mornings are the most reliably peaceful times.

sights & activities

To 'see' Bangkok in a few days, you really need to decide which Bangkok you want to see. If you want the old Thai city – intricate temples, serene 19th-century buildings and grand royal palaces – head to the districts of Ratanakosin, Dusit and Banglamphu.

Ratanakosin is Bangkok's original royal district, its buildings heavy with significance. **Dusit** is a leafy, European-style royal area with intricate palaces, while **Banglamphu** has important temples, as well as the remains of former city fortresses.

Banglamphu is also a destination for new city explorers. The infamous backpacker centre of **Th Khao San** is a magnet for young travellers and lost socks from the laundromat of life, and has great people-watching. The **old farang areas** – around the Oriental Hotel and the Thonburi bank of Mae Nam Chao Phraya opposite – offer insights into the life of a European expat around the turn of the 20th century.

Contemporary Bangkok is centred around Silom, Sukhumvit and Siam, their vast shopping centres surrounded by those symbols of modern life – traffic, billboards and neon lights. For the cheapest bird's-eye view of this area, catch a Skytrain along any of these roads.

Silom is the home of Bangkok's hottest bar scene, some inventive restaurants and the infamous Patpong area, while **Siam** is a fairly soulless temple to retail therapy. Many expats live around **Sukhumvit**, so it's dominated by top-notch restaurants and shops.

If you just want to feel like you're not in Bangkok, you can wander the streets of Chinatown, Little India (or Phahurat, just west of Chinatown) or Little Arabia (located between Sois 3 and 5, Th Sukhumvit).

Off the Beaten Track

With a population density of 3600 people per square kilometre and millions of visitors each year, Bangkok's tracks are well and truly beaten. To get away from it all, take a longtail boat down one of the Thonburi canals; join a meditation class at Wat Mahathat (at least your mind can escape the crowds); or find a quiet bench in Lumphini Park or along the river at Santichaiprakan Park.

Bangkok for Free

These sights won't cost you a measly sateng:

- Wat Mahathat
- Chatuchak Weekend Market (your discipline pending, of course)
- Erawan Shrine
- Monk's Bowl Village
- Museum of the Department of Forensic Medicine
- Congdon Museum of Anatomy
- All the churches

Elegance personified – dancer's costume, Erawan Shrine

TEMPLES & SHRINES

A *wat* is a Buddhist compound, where men or women are ordained as monks or nuns. They're usually major social centres – try to experience a lively temple fair *(ngaan wát)*, held on auspicious dates and celebrated with music and feasting.

City Pillar (2, G3)

Inside this shrine, at the south-eastern corner of Sanam Luang and known as Lak Meuang, is a wooden pillar representing the founding of the new capital on the eastern side of the river. Worshippers make offerings – often by commissioning traditional dancers or occasionally with severed pigs' heads and incense – to the spirit of the pillar, considered the city's guardian.

✉ **cnr Th Ratchadamnoen Nai & Th Lak Meuang, Ratanakosin** 🚌 air-con 6, 7 ⛴ Tha Chang ⑤ free ♿ good

Erawan Shrine (3, C9)

This Brahman shrine is engulfed by a perpetual stream of merit-makers and is thick with the haze of incense smoke, overbur-

Multi-hued Sri Mariamman Hindu temple

dened stalls with garlands and caged birds (releasing them earns merit) and the clanging of traditional musicians. Similarly chaotic circumstances surround its beginnings – it was built to ward off bad luck after mishaps delayed construction of the first Erawan Hotel nearby.

✉ **cnr Th Ploenchit & Th Ratchadamri** 🚈 Chitlom 🚌 air-con 1, 8, 11, 13 ⑤ free ♿ good

Sri Gurusingh Sabha Temple (2, K5)

This sleek and modern Sikh temple (it's kitted out with elevators and marble throughout) is devoted to Guru Granth Sahib, one of the last 10 gurus or teachers. You'll find it down a little alleyway off Th Chakraphet.

✉ **Th Chakraphet,**

Phahurat 🚌 1, 3, 5, 7, 8, 21, 25, 37, 40, 48, 56 ⛴ Tha Saphan Phut ⑤ free ♿ good

Sri Mariamman Temple (3, J4)

The Sri Mariamman Hindu temple is a colourful place of worship in every sense of the word, from the multi-hued main temple built by Tamil immigrants in the 1860s to the eclectic range of people of many faiths and nationalities who come to make offerings. Thais call it Wat Phra Si Kaha Umathewi.

✉ **Th Silom, Bangrak** 🚌 air-con 2, 4, 5, 15 ⑤ free

Wat Benchamabophit (2, C9)

Buddha image buffs find Wat Benchamabophit fascinating. Known as the 'Marble

Buddha image at Wat Benchamabophit

Offerings to the spirit of the pillar, City Pillar Shrine

Temple Etiquette

To ensure you don't insult anybody when visiting temples:

- dress neatly, making sure your legs and shoulders are covered (ie, no sleeveless tops or shorts)
- take your shoes off as you enter a building containing a Buddha image
- respect Buddha images, which are sacred to Thais – don't pose for photos in front of them, touch them or point your feet towards them
- remember that monks aren't supposed to touch or be touched by women

Temple' (it's made of white Carrara marble), it has a collection of 53 Buddha images in all different figures and styles. It was built during Rama V's reign – the temple's central Buddha image contains his ashes – and its cruciform bòt is a pure example of modern wat architecture.
✉ cnr Th Sri Ayuthaya

Roof tiles, Wat Benchamabophit

& Th Phra Ram V, Dusit 🚌 air-con 3 🕐 8am-5.30pm 💲 20B

Wat Bowonniwet

(6, C5) Monks from around the world come to study at Wat Bowonniwet, home to the country's second Buddhist university, Mahamakut University, and the national headquarters of the Thammayut monastic sect. It may be in the midst of ultra-casual Banglamphu but it is a royal wat (the present king was temporarily ordained here) and visitors must dress appropriately.
✉ Th Phra Sumen, Banglamphu 🚤 Tha Banglamphu

Wat Chong Nonsi

(1, J3) In an industrial area south of the city centre, Wat Chong Nonsi is an important Ayuthaya-era temple. Its noted *jataka* murals were painted between 1657 and 1707, and, like the temple itself,

haven't been renovated – making them pure examples of Ayuthaya styles.
✉ off Th Ratchadaphisek, Thanon Tok 🚕 taxi

Wat Intharawihan

(2, C6) This temple at the northern edges of Banglamphu is known for its 32m standing Buddha image in the modern style. Also have a look at the hollow, air-conditioned stupa with a lifelike image of Luang Phaw Toh.
✉ Th Wisut Kasat, Banglamphu 🚤 Tha Thewet 🚌 air-con 3, 6, 17 💲 by donation

Wat Mangkon Kamalawat

(2, K8) Wat Mangkon Kamalawat has a phenomenal energy and its marble floors with lilypad motif must be trampled by hundreds of people daily. Explore its labyrinthine passageways and you'll find endless shrines, surrounded by devotees of Buddhism, Taoism and Confucianism.
✉ Th Charoen Krung,

Entrance to Wat Mangkon Kamalawat

E of Th Ratchawong, Chinatown ⛴ **Tha Ratchawong** $ **free**

Wat Ratchabophit
(2, H4) Commissioned by Rama V soon after he came to the throne, this beautiful temple is decorated with Chinese porcelain. European influences are fairly strong, too – look at the uniforms of the carved guards on the door.
✉ **Th Rajabophit, near cnr of Th Atasadang, Ratanakosin** 🚌 **60** ⛴ **Tha Tien** 🕘 **9am-6pm** $ **free**

Wat Ratchanatda
(2, F6) Rama III built this temple in honour of his granddaughter, but these days it's better known for its vibrant amulet market and its amazing spikey, metal monastery (Loh Prasat), with many passageways and meditation cells at each intersection.
✉ **cnr Th Ratchadamnoen Klang & Th Mahachai** 🚌 **air-con 5** 🕘 **9am-5pm** $ **free**

Buddha statues, Wat Suthat

Jataka murals on the walls of Wat Suthat

Wat Suthat & Giant Swing (2, G5)
Wat Suthat is shrouded in importance – it holds the highest royal temple grade and is home to Brahman priests who perform rites like the Royal Ploughing Ceremony. Inside the high-ceilinged *wíhăan* are intricate jataka murals and Thailand's biggest surviving Sukhothai-era bronze. Just over the road is the Giant Swing (Sao Ching-Cha), the former site of a spectacular Brahman festival.
✉ **Th Bamrung Muang** 🚌 **air-con 8** 🕘 **8.30am-9pm** $ **20B**

Wat Suwannaram
(1, G1) Along Khlong Bankok Noi, Wat Suwannaram is an Ayuthaya-era temple, boasting jataka murals created by two pre-eminent artists of the Rama III era and considered the best remaining temple paintings in the city. But the temple has a dark past – Burmese prisoners-of-war were executed here during King Taksin's era and it was the site of Bangkok's first concrete crematorium.
✉ **Khlong Bangkok Noi, before Th Charan Sanitwong** ⛴ **longtail taxi**

Wat Thammamongkhon
(1, J5) It's a hike out to the outer reaches of Th Sukhumvit, but the sight of the 95m-high *chedi* at Wat Thammamongkhon is pretty incredible. So, too, is the 14-tonne jade Buddha sculpture. The chedi – only a decade old and complete with elevator – comes from a monk's vision of a jade boulder (around the same time one such boulder was discovered in Canada).
✉ **Soi 101, Th Sukhumvit** 🚆 **On Nut, then taxi** 🕘 **9am-5pm** $ **free**

Swingers
The red Giant Swing was built for a dramatic and dangerous Brahman festival, where teams would swing in massive arcs to try to reach a bag of gold hanging from a 15m bamboo pole. So many people died that Rama VII called a halt to the antics, which were held in honour of the Hindu god Shiva.

CHURCHES

Though few in number, Bangkok has some interesting Catholic churches dating back as far as the 17th century. You'll usually find them in the old farang areas – around the Oriental Hotel on the Bangkok side and the former Portugese quarter in Thonburi.

Assumption Cathedral (3, J2)

This shady Catholic church has stunning stained-glass windows and an altar made of marble imported from France. It's in a quiet complex just off Soi Oriental and fronts onto a Bangkok rarity, a small square.

✉ **Soi Oriental, Th Charoen Krung** ☎ **02 234 8556** 🚇 **Saphan Taksin** 🚌 **75, 115, 116** 🚢 **Tha Oriental & hotel shuttle boat from Tha Sathorn** ⑤ **free**

Double-towered facade of Assumption Cathedral

Church of the Immaculate Conception (2, A5)

This Catholic church was built by the Portugese in the 17th century and later taken over by Cambodians fleeing civil war. The current building, overlooking the river, is an 1837 reconstruction of the original church, which is now a museum of holy relics.

✉ **167 Soi Mittakam, Th Samsen, Dusit** ☎ **02 243 2617** 🚢 **Tha Thewet** ⑤ **free**

Church of Santa Cruz (2, L3)

The Church of Santa Cruz is in the thick of what was the old Portugese quarter. The current building was built in 1913 and is known as Wat Kuta Jiin (Chinese Monastic Residence), reflecting the Chinese influences of its architecture.

✉ **Soi Kuti Jiin, Thonburi** 🚢 **Tha Saphan Phut** ⑤ **free**

Holy Rosary Church (3, G2)

Vietnamese and Cambodian Catholics rebuilt this Portugese church over a century ago – you'll see French inscriptions beneath the Stations of the Cross. During Easter celebrations, an old statue of Christ is carried through the streets.

✉ **1318 Th Yotha, near River City** ☎ **02 266 4849** 🚌 **16, 36, 93** 🚢 **Tha Si Phraya** ⑤ **free**

Stained glass window, Assumption Cathedral

The Portuguese in Bangkok

Like many European nations wanting to trade with the legendary city of Ayuthaya, Portugal made its presence felt in the 17th century, even setting up an embassy in the capital. But after Ayuthaya's fall, many Portuguese took land along the river in Bangkok, mostly on the Thonburi side. Their main legacy is a collection of grand Catholic churches.

MUSEUMS & GALLERIES

Some of Bangkok's five-star hotels have impressive and vast collections of contemporary art, especially the Grand Hyatt Erawan and The Landmark Bangkok (pp. 104-5). Pick up a copy of the free monthly *art connection* brochure which lists the latest on galleries and shows.

Ancient Cloth Museum (2, A8)

If you're interested in fashion, you should enjoy a poke around this museum, with its well-annotated collection of royal cloth and royals wearing cloth (Queen Sirikit looks a bit groovy in B&W photos taken in her younger days).
- ✉ Dusit Park, Th Ratchawithi, Dusit
- ☎ 02 281 4715
- 🚌 air-con 10, 16, 18
- 🚤 Tha Thewet
- 🕐 9.30am-4pm
- 💲 50/20B adult/child (free with Grand Palace ticket) 🚻 good

Ban Kamthieng (4, B1)

It was being renovated when we visited, but when it reopens this fascinating ethnological museum will be better than ever. Decorated in the Lanna style, this traditional northern house shows how a Lanna commoner lived.
- ✉ Siam Society, 131 Soi 21 (Soi Asoke), Th Sukhumvit ☎ 02 661 6470 🚇 Asok 🚌 air-con 22, 38, 136
- 🕐 Mon-Sat 9am-5pm
- 💲 100B

Bangkok Doll Factory & Museum (1, G3)

This museum gives you an interesting, if small-scale, insight into Thai national costumes. New and antique dolls (including some delicate, handmade items) dressed in various costumes are displayed around the showroom, while the factory sells a huge range.
- ✉ 85 Soi Ratchataphan, Th Ratchaprarop, Pratunam ☎ 02 245 3008 🚕 taxi 🕐 Mon-Sat 8am-5pm 💲 free

Monk's Bowl Village (2, G7)

Rama I created three villages to make alms bowls for the monks at nearby Wat Saket. Monks still receive food donations in the bowls each morning but there's only one village, an alley wide, where artisans handcraft the metal dishes. They're not always at work, but try your luck – head south on Th Boriphat, then left onto Soi Baan Baht.
- ✉ Soi Baan Baht, Th Bamrung Muang, Phra Nakhon 🚌 air-con 15 🚤 canal taxi down Khlong Saen Saep 🚻 good

National Gallery (6, D2)

This gallery should be so much better than it is. Based in the old mint building, it has collections of traditional and contemporary art, but keep an eye out for temporary exhibitions, which could be more promising, and pieces by Rama VI and King Bhumibol.
- ✉ 4 Th Chao Fa, Banglamphu
- ☎ 02 282 2639
- 🚤 Tha Banglamphu
- 🕐 Wed-Sun 9am-4pm
- 💲 30/10B 🚻 good

Planetarium & Museum of Science (1, H4)

The best thing about the Planetarium & Museum of Science is the emphasis on hands-on involvement. The exhibits aren't wildly exciting, but interesting enough to pass an hour or so. Get an insight into how Thais interpret the skies.
- ✉ between Sois 40 & 42, Th Sukhumvit

Monk's Bowls

It can take an artisan a whole day to hammer a monk's bowl together. The bowls are created from eight pieces of steel (representing Buddha's eightfold path), then fused, polished and coated with black lacquer. Expect to pay around 500B for one.

Art Bars

If you want to see cutting-edge modern art, check out the 'art bars' (bar-restaurants with changing art exhibitions on the walls), where you can value-add to your cultural experience with a drink or top Thai meal. Try places like About Studio/About Cafe (p. 92), Bangkok Bar (the Th Phra Sumen one; p. 75), Commé (p. 75) and Eat Me (p. 85).

☎ 02 392 5952 🚇 Ekamai ⏰ Tues-Sun 8.30am-4.30pm ⑤ 40B, children 20B

Prasart Museum

(off map 1) This museum isn't in Bangkok but we've included it because Prasart Vongsakul's collection of traditional buildings and antiques, set in lush gardens, is a must for any diehard art and architecture fan. It's tricky to get to so call ahead for directions and let them know you're coming.
✉ 9 Soi Krungthepkretha 4a, Th Krung Thepkretha, Bang Kapi ☎ 02 379 3601 🚌 93 ⏰ Tues-Sun 10am-3pm ⑤ 300B

Royal Elephant Museum

(2, A8) Thais considered albinism auspicious, so all white elephants are considered royal property (King Bhumibol keeps one at his palace). Dusit had two stables for keeping white elephants, though today they house this museum, which has displays explaining the ranks of elephants and their important role in Thai society. It's quite interesting – and certainly no white elephant.
✉ Dusit Park ☎ 02 628 6300 🚌 air-con 10, 16, 18 🚢 Tha Thewet ⏰ 9.30am-4pm ⑤ 50/20B adult/child (free with Grand Palace ticket) ♿ good

Rotunda Gallery

(3, H5) This gallery in the Neilson-Hays Library sometimes scores good temporary exhibitions. It's a small space but it attracts a varied bunch of artists, from photographers to pen-and-ink types.
✉ Neilson-Hays Library, 195 Th Surawong ☎ 02 233 1731 🚇 Chong Nonsi 🚌 1, 16, 35, 36, 75, 93 ⏰ Tues, Thur, Fri & Sat 9.30am-4pm, Wed 9.30am-5pm, Sun 9.30am-2pm ⑤ free

Royal Thai Air Force Museum

(1, C5) This museum is strictly for the aficionado, who'll probably relish spending a day out around Don Meuang. The museum, near wing 6 at the airport, is truly world-class, with some rare historic planes, including WWII fighter craft.
✉ Th Phahonyothin, Don Meuang ☎ 02 534 1853 📧 www.rtaf.mi.th/museum 🚆 suburban train to Don Meuang 🚌 air-con 4, 10, 13, 29 ⏰ Mon-Fri 8am-4pm, Sat-Sun 8.30am-4.30pm ⑤ free

Sangaroon House

(4, B1) Thai architect Sangaroon Ratagasikorn studied under Frank Lloyd Wright in the USA. When he returned to Thailand he donated the traditional-style Sangaroon House and his collection of folk utensils to the Siam Society. Like its neighbour, Ban Kamthieng, Sangaroon House is under renovation.
✉ Siam Society, 131

Don't forget to visit the Royal Elephant Museum.

Soi 21 (Soi Asok), Th Sukhumvit ☎ 02 661 6470 🚇 Asok 🚌 air-con 22, 38, 136 ⏰ Mon-Sat 9am-5pm 💲 100B

Silpakorn Art Gallery (2, G2)

Silpakorn University is renowned for its exceptional Fine Arts Department, considered the best in Bangkok. Keep an eye on the list-

Art for the Other Side

As you walk down Trok Itsaranuphap in Chinatown, keep an eye out for the funerary art shops, crammed with paper cars, designer shirts, 'passports to heaven' and even houses for loved ones to take with them into the next life.

ings press for upcoming temporary exhibitions and take a look through the excellent art bookshop next door.
✉ 31 Th Na Phra Lan,

Ratanakosin ☎ 02 221 5874-5 🚌 air-con 3, 6, 8, 12, 44 ⛴ Tha Chang ⏰ Mon-Fri 9am-7pm, Sat 10am-5pm 💲 charges can apply

Thailand Cultural Centre (1, F4)

This top-class, multipurpose arts venue often has temporary art exhibitions, as well as musical and drama shows. Check its website for updates.
✉ Th Ratchadapisek (btw Soi Tiam Ruammit & Th Din Daeng), Huay Kwang ☎ 02 247 0028 🚕 taxi 🌐 www.thai culturalcenter.com 💲 charges can apply ♿ good

Nothing finer – exhibits at Silpakorn Art Gallery

NOTABLE BUILDINGS

Baiyoke Sky Hotel (1, G3)

Wait til nightfall to zoom to the top of this hotel, the nation's biggest tower with 84 floors. During the day the visibility can be poor because of the pollution but during the night the lights positively twinkle.
✉ 22 Th Ratchaprarop, Pratunam ☎ 02-656 3000 📧 baiyoke@ mozart.inet.co.th, www.baiyokehotels.co .th 🚌 air-con 4, 13, 15, 38, 139, 140 ⏰ 10.30am-10.30pm 💲 120B ♿ good

Bank of Asia (3, K6)

During the crazy 80s, when no building project was too outlandish or expensive, architect Sumet Jumsai created his now-famous 'robot building' for the Bank of Asia. Few were keen on it at the time, but now it seems quaint and retro.
✉ cnr Th Sathon Tai & Soi Pikun 🚇 Chong Nonsi 🚌 air-con 15, 67 💲 free

Chitlada Palace (2, B10)

King Bhumibol, Queen Sirikit and some royal white elephants live

Bank of Asia's famous 'robot building'

Can Phra Sumen Fort withstand the traveller onslaught?

at Chitlada Palace, but, obviously, it's not open to the public. It's actually quite difficult to spot the palace proper but you should be able to spy some of the king's agricultural projects on the grounds.
⊠ **cnr Th Ratwithi & Th Rama V, Dusit** 🚌 **air-con 10, 16, 18**

Democracy Monument (2, F5)
Four-pronged Democracy Monument holds a key place in Bangkok's political history. Built to commemorate the transition from absolute monarchy to constitutional monarchy in 1932, the monument is the natural home of pro-democracy rallies, including the tragic demonstrations of 1992 that turned bloody at the hands of the military.
⊠ **cnr Th**

Ratchadamnoen Klang & Th Din So 🚣 **Tha Banglamphu**

Oriental Hotel (2, P9)
Quite simply, the Oriental is the most famous hotel in Bangkok. Its new wings are, from the outside, pretty unattractive, but the original building – the white-shuttered and colonial-style Author's Lounge – shows why this hotel was the tropical pit-stop of choice for Joseph Conrad, Noel Coward, Graham Greene, Gore Vidal and Barbara Cartland.
⊠ **48 Soi Oriental, Th Charoen Krung, Bangrak** ☎ **02 236 0400** 📧 **www.mandarin oriental.com** 🚌 **Saphan Taksin** 🚌 **75, 115, 116** 🚣 **Tha Oriental & hotel shuttle boat from Tha Sathorn** 💲 **free** ♿ **good**

Phra Sumen Fort
(6, B3) Rock-solid and blindingly white, Phra Sumen Fort in Santichiprakan Park is one of Banglamphu's most recognisable landmarks. Built in 1783, the imposing octagonal building was one of many fortresses along Khlong Banglamphu designed to defend the city against invasion. These days, it's a passive observer to the traveller onslaught of Banglamphu.
⊠ **cnr Th Phra Athit & Th Phra Sumen, Banglamphu** 🚌 **air-con 6** 🚣 **Tha Banglamphu** 💲 **free** ♿ **good**

The Original Siamese Twins
If it wasn't for an English trader taking a quiet stroll along the river one afternoon in 1824, Siamese twins would probably be known by an entirely different name. Robert Hunter spied an eight-limbed and two-headed creature in the water and was astonished to discover it was two conjoined 13-year-old boys, called Chang and Eng. The brothers became celebrities in the best freak show tradition of the times, touring Europe and the USA, and featuring in PT Barnum's museum. They eventually settled in North Carolina, where they married sisters, produced 22 children and died within hours of each other.

Democracy Monument – memories of 1932 and 1992

PARKS & GARDENS

Some Bangkok residents confess to the odd fantasy of rolling on a patch of lawn, such is the pitiful amount of park space in the city. At least the few parks are well utilised, whether it's for aerobics classes, family gatherings or marketplaces.

Benjasiri Park (4, D4)
In summer this park, built to honour Queen Sirikit's 60th birthday, hosts many open-air events. It's built around an ornamental lake, with most of the surrounding lawn space taken by canoodling couples and teenage mating rituals-in-progress. But there's a good playground and places for kids to skateboard and play basketball. If you're lucky you might spy a *tàkrâw* game.
✉ **btw Sois 22 & 24, Th Sukhumvit**
🚇 **Phrom Phong**
🚌 **air-con 1, 2, 8, 11, 13, 38** ⏲ **5am-8pm**
⑤ **free** ♿ **excellent**

Chatuchak Park
(1, E3) Most people visit this park unintentionally – one of its corners is devoted to the Chatuchak Weekend Market – but it is worth a Skytrain trip for some solitude. There's a big kids' playground and sculptures dotted throughout its vast grounds.
🚇 **Bang Seu**
⏲ **5am-8pm** ⑤ **free**
♿ **excellent**

Santichaiprakan Park
(6, B3) It's a tiny patch of greenery interspersed with much concrete but somehow this park has got a soul. Every evening, it's bustling with families, travellers attempting circus tricks and an amusing open-air aerobics class. The riverside pathway, heading (and gradually being expanded) southwards, makes for a serene *passeggiata*.
✉ **cnr Th Phra Athit & Th Phra Sumen, Banglamphu** 🚌 **air-con 6**
🚤 **Tha Banglamphu**
⑤ **free** ♿ **good**

Elephants

It's a difficult, transitional time for Thai elephants. Their numbers are shrinking and modern problems have put many of them (and their handlers) out of a job. Some have been steered into new career directions like, most famously, painting – for a few months they were the darlings of the art world.

Benjasiri isn't Thai for a walk in the park.

QUIRKY BANGKOK

Bangkok itself is one big quirky attraction. But there's plenty that stands out as particularly curious, even after you've seen the snake-blood stalls at Lumphini Park.

Congdon Museum of Anatomy (2, F1)

This anatomical museum can be unsettling but quite fascinating. It's best known for its many exhibits of Siamese twins (think twice about visiting if you don't think you can handle seeing preserved dead babies) and incredible displays of arterial and nervous systems.
✉ 3rd fl, Anatomical Building, Siriraj Hospital, Th Phrannok, Bangkok Noi ☎ 02 419 7035 🚤 Tha Rot Fai ⏰ Mon-Fri 9am-4pm ⑤ free ♿ good

House of Gems (2, P9)

The name House of Gems is certainly an interesting sales pitch for a shop that claims to sell dinosaur droppings. If you look in the window, some delicate, dry cross-sections will teach you the subtle difference between the 'gems' of a carnivorous dinosaur, compared to its herbivorous friends. Don't say we didn't tell you that there's nothing you can't buy in Bangkok.
✉ 1218 Th Charoen

Other Oddities

Other places to experience Bangkok at its most curious include Lumphini Park in the morning (p. 21), Chatuchak Weekend Market's wildlife section (p. 15) and Chinatown at any time of the day or night (p. 16).

Lingam (Phallus) Shrine

Krung, near Th Surawong, Bangrak
🚇 Saphan Taksin
🚌 75, 115, 116
⚓ Tha Oriental
⏰ 10am-8pm

Lingam (Phallus) Shrine (3, B11)

This little shrine at the back of the Hilton was built for the spirit of a nearby tree. But then all these wooden phalluses start appearing, to the extent that it's now like a dense wooden penis forest. Many women come to the shrine to pray for fertility.
✉ Nai Loet Park, Th Withayu ⚓ canal taxi to Nailert ⑤ free

Museum of Forensic Medicine (2, 1E)

Seriously, do not come to this museum with a full stomach or if the slightest drop of blood makes you faint. It has preserved body parts that have been crushed, shot, stabbed and raped, with grisly before-and-after photos, as well as the entire remains of a notorious Thai murderer. The small shrines next to babies'

remains are sobering.
✉ 2nd fl, Forensic Pathology Bldg, Siriraj Hospital, Th Phrannok, Bangkok Noi ⚓ Tha Rot Fai ⏰ Mon-Fri 9am-4pm ⑤ free ♿ good

Queen Saovabha Memorial Institute (3, F7)

It's touristy and completely compelling. This snake farm, one of only a few worldwide, was established in 1923 to breed snakes for antivenenes. The snake feeding and milking shows are a nice sideline, where snake handlers educate and freak out visitors about Thailand's venomous snakes by letting the baddest ones loose (don't fret, you're safe in the stands).
✉ cnr Th Rama IV & Th Henri Dunant ☎ 02 252 0161 🚇 Sala Daeng ⏰ Mon-Fri 8.30am-4.30pm, Sat-Sun 8.30am-noon; shows Mon-Fri 11am & 2.30pm, Sat-Sun 11am ⑤ 70B ♿ good

Wat Prayoon (2, M4)

Near the old Portuguese quarter in Thonburi is this unusual temple complex. An artificial hill, built under the orders of Rama III, is littered with curious miniature shrines, and little temples, stupa and prang. There's also a cute turtle pond.
✉ beside Memorial Bridge, near Wat Arun ⚓ Tha Saphan Phut ⑤ free

BANGKOK FOR CHILDREN

During kite-flying season, head for the parks and the action of the skies. But when it's hot and humid and the kids are cranky, your best option is probably one of the many air-conditioned shopping centres with amusements galore.

Central Chidlom
(3, C10) If your teenagers are champing at the bit, take them to the 4th floor of this department store. It's got a skateboard ramp and a basketball rink for shooting practice.
✉ 1027 Th Ploenchit, Pratunam ☎ 02 233 6930-9 🚇 Chitlom 🚌 air-con 1, 8, 11, 13 🕐 10am-9pm ⑤ free ♿ good

Young girl absorbed in the art of painting

Dusit Zoo (2, A9)
The peaceful grounds of this zoo once hosted Rama V's botanical garden. It would be quite easy to spend a day here, as there are oodles of eateries, a playground and a big lake for paddleboating. The animal storage areas are not the most modern.
✉ Th Rama V, btw Th Ratwithi & Th Si Ayuthaya, Dusit ☎ 02 281 2000 🚌 air-con 10, 16, 18 ⛴ Tha Thewet 🕐 9am-6pm ⑤ 40/30B ♿ excellent

Paintings by local children on the walls at Dusit Zoo

Jamboree (4, D4)
A corner of this glamorous shopping centre is for the rugrats. There's a gym-style playground, coin-operated Godzillas to ride, little cars to drive plus loads of video games.
✉ 3rd fl, The Emporium, btw Sois 22 & 24 ☎ 02 664 8000 🚇 Phrom Phong 🚌 air-con 1, 2, 8, 11, 13, 38 🕐 Mon-Fri 10.30am-10pm, Sat & Sun 10am-10pm ♿ good

Kim Bowl (3, C6)
Thai teenagers crowd this bowling alley at all hours of the day and night. The cost varies, depending what time of the day you play, but the most a game will cost you is 90B (80B students).
✉ 8th fl, Mah Boon Krong, cnr Th Phra Ram I & Th Phayathai, Siam ☎ 02 255 9500 🚇 National Stadium 🚌 air-con 1, 2, 29, 141 🕐 10am-1am ⑤ 90B

Siam Park (1, D5)
You'll probably be fighting to have the first go on some of the waterslides, which come in all shapes and sizes. If your kids are big then leave them to the slides or amusement rides while you kick back on the artificial beach complete with not-so-gnarly 'surf'.
✉ 99 Th Serathai, Khannayao ☎ 02 919 7200 🚌 27 from Victory Monument 🕐 Mon-Fri 10am-6pm, Sat & Sun 9am-7pm ⑤ 200/100B

Babysitters
It might be hard finding a sitter if you're not staying in one of the better hotels – most Bangkok residents use extended family or maids rather than a babysitter – but few places will bat an eyelid if you bring the kids with you.

Safari World (1, D5)

Safari World bills itself as the 'World of Happiness'. It's undoubtedly fun and you do get two top attractions at this vast wildlife centre – the drive-through Safari Park, with African and Asian animals, and walk-through Marine Park, with dolphin shows – which could certainly make you happy. Set aside a day to see everything in this open-air zoo.

✉ 99 Th Ramindra, Minburi ☎ 02 518 1000 e www.safari world.com 🚍 27 from Victory Monument, then sawngtháew ⊙ 9am-5pm ⑤ 400/300B

World Trade Centre skaters feel on top of the world.

World Ice-Skating
(3, B9) You feel like you're in the 'burbs, or at least an American teen movie, at this ice-skating rink at the very top of the World Trade Centre. It's a functional rink with no frills but lots of corny music.

✉ 7th fl, World Trade Centre, cnr Th Phra Ram I & Th Ratchadamri 🚉 Chitlom 🚍 air-con 4, 5, 11, 13, 15 ⚓ canal taxi to Nailert ⊙ Mon-Fri 10am-8.30pm, Sat-Sun 10am-2.45pm & 3.30-8.30pm ⑤ 130B

MEDITATION

At temples, instruction in Theravada Buddhist meditation and accommodation are free, though you should give a donation. If you are undertaking a retreat, or course longer than a few days, you are expected not to leave the compound for the entire time, so bring clothes and toiletries.

Wat Mahathat (2, F2)

Wat Mahathat's International Buddhist Meditation Centre is where most Westerners study *satipatthana* (mindfulness) meditation in Bangkok. Classes are held three times daily and are a mix of experienced and beginner meditators. Some monks speak English, though there's usually a Western monk or long-term resident who can translate.

✉ section 5, 3 Th Maharaj, Ratanakosin ☎ 02 222 6011 🚍 air-con 3, 6 ⚓ Tha Maharat ⑤ free ♿ limited

World Fellowship of Buddhists (4, D4)

On the first Sunday of the month, this centre of Theravada Buddhism hosts meditation classes in English from 2pm to 5.30pm. The fellowship also holds interesting forums on Buddhist issues.

✉ Benjasiri Park, Soi 24, Th Sukhumvit ☎ 02 661 1284 e www.buddhanet .net/wfb.htm 🚉 Phrom Phong 🚍 air-con 1, 2, 8, 11, 13, 38 ⑤ free

Meditation Mores

You'll be expected to wear white robes when studying meditation at a temple. You should also attend the opening ceremony, when you should provide offerings of incense, candles or fruit to your teacher. You should also attend the closing ceremony at which you formally thank your teacher. The concept of respect for your teacher is of paramount importance.

TRADITIONAL MASSAGE

The going rate for a traditional Thai massage at these places is 300B for 1hr and 400B for two, though increasing competition may push these prices down. Many people also recommend the massages at the Thai herbal medicine shops near Thammasat University which are even cheaper.

Buathip Thai Massage (3, D13)

Buathip has long been known for its blind masseurs, who will give you a strong and intuitive treatment. It's a low-key place favoured by Thai regulars and expats.
✉ **4/1-2 Soi 5, Th Sukhumvit** ☎ **02 251 2627** 🚇 **Nana** 🚌 **air-con 1, 8 , 11, 13**
🕐 **10am-midnight**
♿ **limited**

Marble House (3, G7)

Don't worry that Marble House is in the middle of the sleazy Thaniya scene. The work of its traditional

How to Win Friends

Most of the masseurs pulling and pummeling your muscles honed their skills at the Wat Pho massage school (2, J3; ☎ 02 225 4771). You can study their secrets in a 10-day traditional massage course (3hrs a day) or, if your time is limited, a 9hr foot massage course.

masseurs is so highly respected that it doesn't need to sell sex like everyone else around here. Its air-conditioned teak rooms make the massages even more restorative.
✉ **37/18-19 Soi Surawong Plaza, Th Surawong, Silom** ☎ **02 235 3529** 🚇 **Sala**

Thai Massage

You've put your cotton pyjamas on and you've laid down on the mattress, which is lying on a raised wooden platform. What next? Something that's like a cross between a yoga session, reflexology massage and a workout with the chiropractor. Thais take their massage seriously (the national health department used to have an official massage section) and consider it an important part of holistic health, using it to relax and prevent disease.

Daeng 🚌 **air-con 2, 4, 5, 15** 🕐 **10am-midnight**

Wat Pho (2, J3)

Most travellers come to Wat Pho for their first massage. There's no doubt the massages are authentic but you can feel like you're on a production line. Try the new, flash air-conditioned massage centre, which you have to book through the main office.
✉ **Th Chetuphon Rd, Ratanakosin** ☎ **02 222 2587** 🚌 **air-con 1, 7, 8** ⛴ **Tha Tien** 🕐 **8am-5pm** ♿ **limited**

Winwan (3, C13)

Underestimate the diminutive women masseurs here at your peril. Before you know it, they'll be suspending you in mid-air with just their legs and still be managing to crack jokes with the masseur next to them while you huff and puff. The surroundings aren't salubrious but the massages are excellent.
✉ **btw Sois 1 & 3, Th Sukhumvit** ☎ **02 251 7467** 🚇 **Nana** 🚌 **air-con 1, 8 , 11, 13**
🕐 **10am-11pm**
♿ **good**

THAI COOKING SCHOOLS

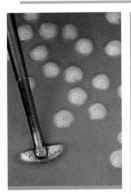

Benjarong Restaurant at Dusit Thani (3, G8)

If you don't have a rowdy Friday night, you could try the Saturday morning classes run by the Benjarong restaurant's head chef. The classes, which can be taken individually or as part of a 12-part course, are hands-on and based on dishes served at the restaurant. Best of all, you get to eat your creations for lunch.

✉ Dusit Thani, cnr Th Silom & Th Phra Ram IV, Silom
☎ 02 236 6400
🚇 Sala Daeng

Mrs Balbir's Restaurant (3, D14)

Inbetween running her restaurant (pp. 81-2) and hosting a cooking show on UBC, the perpetually on-the-move Mrs Balbir teaches one-day Thai cooking classes. You can book private sessions or see if you can get in with a group. Even more fun are her tours to fresh-produce markets, usually to Chatuchak or Khlong Toey, where she teaches her proteges about Thai ingredients.

✉ 155/18 Soi 11/1, Th Sukhumvit
☎ 651 0498 🚇 Nana
🚌 air-con 1, 8, 11, 13

Nipa Thai Restaurant at Landmark Hotel (3, D13)

You don't have to do the full-week course at this top-notch restaurant — get a copy of the lesson selection and choose the day/s which feature dishes you fancy, such as *kài hàw bai toey* (marinated chicken in pandanus leaf) and *yam thàley* (spicy seafood salad). All students get a free spice box, recipe book and meal at the restaurant.

✉ btw Sois 6 & 8, Th

Sukhumvit ☎ 02 254 0404 🚇 Nana 🚌 air-con 1, 8, 11, 13

Oriental Hotel Cooking Centre (2, P8)

Avid chefs might find the hands-off approach a bit frustrating though you still learn a helluva lot by watching the Oriental's top people in action. Morning sessions are held daily, but if you want to complete a longer course, try the decadent, but pricey, weekly package, including classes, meals, accommodation and little luxuries like spa treatments and limousine transfers.

✉ 48 Th Oriental, Bangrak ☎ 02 437 6211 📧 reserve -orbkk@mohg.com, www.mandarinorient al.com ⛴ free shuttle boat from Oriental Hotel

DAY SPAS

These days, every hotel seems to be opening up a day spa, but many take liberties with the label. What you think might be 2hrs in heaven might just as likely be 120mins on a rickety bed with substandard, even unhygienic equipment. We can guarantee that the places listed here are all class.

Banyan Tree Spa

(3, J9) You wind your way along pebbled pathways to your private spa suite, in a traditional Thai design and decorated with floating orchid bowls and carvings. The Balinese Boreh is the treatment of choice – you are treated to 3hrs of deep-tissue massage, a body 'wrap' in warming spices and then a carrot rub.

✉ 20th & 21st fls, Banyan Tree, 21/100 Th Sathorn Tai, Silom
☎ 02 679 1200
e spa-bangkok@ banyantree.com, www.banyantree.com
🚊 Sala Daeng
🚌 air-con 15, 67
🕐 9am-10pm
♿ good

Grande Spa & Fitness Club (3, E15)

The Sheraton's spa is small, dark and intimate, with low roofs. Each of the 11 teak rooms, including a few massage suites for couples, is self-contained, with a shower and dressing room. Loll back in one of the cavernous hydrotherapy baths and detox to your heart's content.

✉ Sheraton Grande Sukhumvit, 250 Th Sukhumvit, btw Sois 12 & 14, Khlong Toey
☎ 02 653 0333
e grande.sukhumvit@ luxurycollection.com, www.luxurycollection .com/grandesukhumvit
🚊 Asok 🚌 air-con 1, 8, 11, 13 🕐 8am-10pm
♿ good

Oriental Spa luxury – you little beauty!

Oriental Spa Thai Health & Beauty Centre (2, P8)

When jetlag hits, you have no option but to call in The Revitaliser, this spa's legendary treatment which pummels, rubs and soothes the nasties from your system and turns you into a human being again. When it opened in 1993, the Oriental was Thailand's first spa and has won countless prestigous awards since.

✉ 48 Soi Oriental, Th Charoen Krung, Bangrak (over river from hotel) ☎ 02 439 7613 e www.man darinoriental.com
🚢 free shuttle from Oriental Hotel 🕐 9am-10pm ♿ good

Music to Your Ears

During the cool season, the Bangkok Symphony Orchestra plays free concerts in Lumphini Park (p. 21) every Sunday from 5pm. Traditional dancers perform at the two big city shrines, Erawan (p. 33) and Lak Meuang (p. 33), as well as at Vimanmek Teak Mansion (p. 26) daily at 10.30am and 2pm.

Traditional dancers performing at Erawan Shrine.

KEEPING FIT

As many locals will attest, keeping fit in Bangkok is not easy – there just aren't that many facilities in the inner city. Joggers take to the paths of Lumphini Park or Dusit Park, while in the outer, outer suburbs are plenty of golf courses to satisfy any budding Tiger Woods out there. See Out & About for details about organised bike rides.

With space so tight, 50m or even 25m swimming pools in the inner city are rare – and often the best ones are part of private clubs like the British Club and Royal Bangkok Sports Club, where there's a waiting list for the pricey membership.

Central Tennis Court Co (3, H10)
There are five hard courts at this complex, just off Th Sathon Tai. If your backhand slice needs a bit of work, you can arrange for some coaching. Book for the busy afterwork times.
✉ **13/1 Soi Attakranprasit, Th Sathon Tai** ☎ **02 213 1909** 🚇 **Sala Daeng** 🚌 **air-con 15, 67** ⏰ **Mon-Fri 6am-10pm, Sat-Sun 11am-9pm** 💲 **100-200B/hr**

Department of Physical Education (3, C5) The membership fees to use the pool here are so cheap that, if you're a keen swimmer, it's worthwhile joining up, even if

Park Life
You have more exercise options if you stay near a park, plus you probably won't have to spend any money. Lumphini Park (3, G8) has an outdoor gym (the scene is very serious), as well as plenty of tai chi classes you can join in with. If you're not shy, join in with the crowds doing free open-air aerobics classes at Santichaiprakan Park (6, B3), Sanam Luang (2, F3) and Lumphini.

you only visit a few times.
✉ **National Stadium, Th Phra Ram I** ☎ **02 215 1535** 🚇 **National Stadium** 🚌 **air-con 8** 🚤 **canal taxi to Ratchathewi** 💲 **300B/yr membership, 25B/hr**

Fitness First (3, D13)
This brand-new gym has an amazing array of services for the price, including pilates, yoga and boxing classes, a free juice bar, a video library and gleaming equipment. It's in the Landmark Bangkok's building but isn't affiliated with the hotel.
✉ **4th fl, The Landmark Bangkok, 138 Th Sukhumvit (btw Sois 4 & 6)** ☎ **02 237 0777** 🚇 **Nana** 🚌 **air-con 1, 8, 11, 13** 💲 **400B/day**

Royal Dusit Golf Club (2, D9) This golf club is

convenient because it's close to town and open to nonmembers, though the course isn't particularly big (it's inside the Royal Turf Club's racetrack). Check the papers for race days, when the golf course is shut.
✉ **Royal Turf Club, 183 Th Phitsanulok, Dusit** ☎ **02 280 0020-5** 🚌 **air-con 9** 💲 **210B (green fees), 80B per round**

Sarn Saeng-Arun Ashram (3, J5)
This ashram, run by a former Thai movie star, offers the most centrally located yoga classes, but you'll need to be quite experienced or speak a bit of Thai to get any benefit.
✉ **64 Soi 10, Th Sathon Tai** ☎ **02 237 0800** 🚇 **Chong Nonsi** 💲 **150B/hr**

Sports Heroes
Thailand is woefully lacking in international sports stars, which is probably why the Thais love to claim American golfer Tiger Woods – whose mother is Thai – as their own. Thai boxer Somluck Khamsing won the country's first ever Olympic gold medal in Atlanta in 1996.

out & about

WALKING TOURS
Chinatown to Little India

From colourful Wat Mangkon Kamalawat ❶ follow one of Chinatown's main arteries, Th Charoen Krung, eastwards until you hit Trok Itsaranuphap, or Soi 16. This raucous laneway is lined with food shops, intense with smells and elbow-to-elbow with locals. Look out for the paper funerary art shops on the left-hand side and grab a dim sum snack from a stall to munch along the way. Turn right into Sampeng Lane, once one of Bangkok's seediest streets but now the home of kitchenware, food, toy and clothing shops. You know you're getting closer to Phahurat, or Little India, when fabric shops start to dominate. When you meet Th Chakraphet, cross the road and turn left. To your right are laneways leading into Phahurat Market ❷ and its rolls of fabric. Clothing and Indian snack stalls nudge you from the left-hand side. Farther down, at the end of a laneway, is Sri Gurusingh Sabha Temple ❸, where local Sikhs worship. About 100m before the river, the road curves around a temple, then heads west. Over the road is the Phra Buddha Yodfa ❹ monument. Keep on walking and the heady aromas of Pak Khlong's flower and vegetable market ❺ should hit you within 50m.

SIGHTS & HIGHLIGHTS
Sampeng Market (p. 62)
Phahurat Market (pp. 61-2)
Sri Gurusingh Sabha Temple (p. 33)
Pak Khlong Market (p. 61)

Traditionally decorated entrance to Chinatown temple, Sampeng Lane

distance 2.5km   **duration** 2hrs
▶ **start** Wat Mangkon Kamalawat;
　🚕 take a taxi
● **end** 🚢 Tha Ratchini

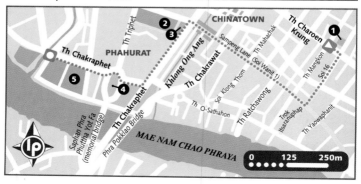

Dusit

This walk takes you through the royal Dusit buildings, set in European-style manicured gardens with fountains. You may have to pay a fee (50/20B adult/child, free with Grand Palace ticket) to enter, but you can wander through the museums in the beautiful former homes of Rama V and his family. Go through the stone gateway at the Th Ratchawithi entrance. On your right are the royal carriage buildings ❶. Follow the main pathway and take the bridge on your left. Pass the house holding an ancient clock collection and take the left-hand path to the Ancient Cloth Museum ❷, a collection of antique and royal textiles. Prehistoric Ban Chiang pottery is stored in the museum farther along. The cafe close by sells drinks and snacks. Cross the bridge and head to Abhisek Dusit Throne Hall ❸ and the Support museum. Across the canal is the Vimanmek Teak Mansion ❹, but to go inside you need the main entry, back across the bridge – past houses with the king's photographic works – and just off the main pathway. Take the main pathway southwards to the end, noting the green Tamnak Ho Residential Hall ❺ and pink Suan Si Rue Du Residential Hall ❻.

SIGHTS & HIGHLIGHTS

Vimanmek Teak Mansion (p. 26)
Abhisek Dusit Throne Hall & Support museum (p. 14)
Ancient Cloth Museum (p. 37)
Ban Chiang Museum
Tamnak Ho Residential Hall
Suan Si Rue Du Residential Hall

Vimanmek Teak Mansion

---

distance 1.5km **duration** 1hr
▶ **start** Th Ratchawithi ⬜ air-con 10, 16, 18
● **end** Th Sri Ayuthaya ⬜ air-con 3

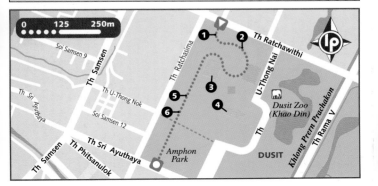

Ratanakosin

You might like to dress modestly for this walk, only because you'll probably want to explore the royal buildings and wáts along the way. Start at the home of Bangkok's city spirit, Lak Meuang (❶; or City Pillar), on the south-eastern corner of Sanam Luang. Walk down Th Sanam-chai, along the walls of the Grand Palace and Wat Phra Kaew ❷; to visit this complex, enter on Th Na Phra Lan). After 500m, turn right onto Th Chetuphon, where you'll find the entrance to Wat Pho ❸, Bangkok's oldest temple and home of traditional Thai massage (handy if your feet are already

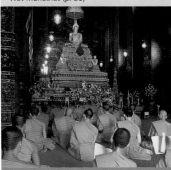

Monks at morning prayers, Wat Pho

distance 3km **duration** 2½hrs
▶ **start** 🚢 Tha Chang
● **end** 🚢 Tha Phra Chan

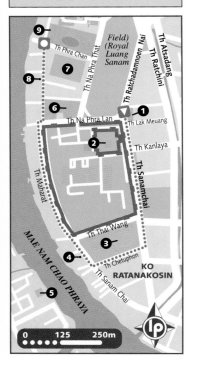

sore). Next turn right onto Th Maharat, perhaps stopping at the Tha Tien market ❹, and then turn left onto Th Thai Wang, with many early Ratanakosin-era shophouses. Wat Arun ❺ and its porcelain-encrusted *prang* is just a 2B ferry trip across the river away. Heading up Th Maharat again, you hit Th Na Phra Lan, with good noodle shops and the entry to Silpakorn University ❻. Still on Th Maharat, you pass Wat Mahathat ❼ – where you can get your fortune told – on your right and the amulet market on your left ❽. Reaching Th Phra Chan, turn left to find Tha Phra Chan or turn right to start exploring Thammasat University ❾.

Old Banglamphu

From Democracy Monument ❶, follow Th Din So past the old shop-houses, many dating from Rama V and Rama VII times. The area was first settled during the reign of Rama IV by farmers and merchants from Ayuthaya. As you turn onto Th Phra Sumen, you'll hit a spate of nationalistic shops, selling Thai flags and Thai royal family paraphernalia. The left-hand side of the street becomes dominated by the long white wall of Wat Bowonniwet ❷. Look over the road to see a former city gate ❸. Soon the imposing white Phra Sumen Fort ❹ and the surrounding Santichaiprakan Park ❹ loom into view. Stop by Roti-Mataba (see p. 77) for a takeaway snack to eat by the river. From here you can choose to follow the riverside walkway down to the Bangkok Tourist Bureau or take Th Phra Sumen's continuation, Th Phra Athit, to see some historic buildings. The impressive Ban Phra Athit ❺ on your left dates from the Ratanakosin era, as does the Buddhist Society of Thailand ❻ building on your right a little farther down the street. The main sight in this street, though, is Ban Maliwan ❼, now home to the UN Food & Agriculture Organization. Walk under Saphan Phra Pin Klao and you're at the tourist bureau.

SIGHTS & HIGHLIGHTS

Democracy Monument (p. 40)
Wat Bowonniwet (p. 34)
Phra Sumen Fort (p. 40)
Santichaiprakan Park (p. 41)

Detail on temple wall, Wat Bowonniwet

---

distance 1.8km **duration** 1hr
▶ **start** Democracy Monument ▣ air-con 3, 6, 9, 11, 12, 15, 17, 39, 44, 68, 153
● **end** ▣ Tha Banglamphu

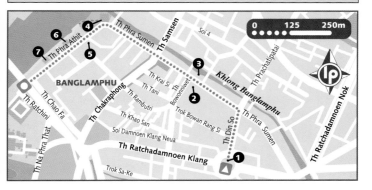

EXCURSIONS

Ayuthaya (7, A4)

During its heady four centuries as the capital of Siam, Ayuthaya was one of South-East Asia's most sophisticated – and, reputedly, glittering – cities. But a thorough sacking by the Burmese abruptly ended that legendary golden age, leaving Ayuthaya in ruins. Today you can wander between the remnants of the temples that make up this Unesco World Heritage site, but you'll need the help of a hired bicycle (30B a day), *túk-túk* or *sawngthăew* (30B per trip to any destination, or 200B per hour) to cover the big distances between them in a day.

Wat Phra Mahathat (30B) has an impressive prang, while **Wat Ratburana** (30B) has a stupa in the Singhalese style. Climb the stairs up the Wat Ratburana's main prang to find the steep stairs into the crypt storing murals. In 1957, it was broken into by robbers, who stole some objects intended for interment (some were recovered and they, like many Ayuthaya gems, are at Bangkok's National Museum). Nearby **Wat Thammikarat** (free) has stone lions and *chedi* ruins. **Wat Phra Si Sanphet** (30B) was the biggest temple of its time, as its three striking chedi in the classic Ayuthaya style, built to store the remains of three different kings, will remind you. The biggest Buddha image in the world lives at **Wat Phanan Choeng** (20B), a working temple built before Ayuthaya became the national capital. Its Buddha image is gleaming and golden, with earlobes the size of Malibu surfboards. **Wat Yai Chai Mongkhon's** (20B) white reclining Buddha has graced many a postcard and reclines in peaceful, shady gardens.

Sunset over Wat Phra Si Sanphet

The Elephant Walk

After a hard day's work of lugging people around, Ayuthaya's elephants knock off around 5pm and begin their slow amble homewards. You can watch them walking in line from their 'office' on Th Pa Thon to the elephant kraal via Th Si Sanphet and Th Chee Kun.

Damnoen Saduak Floating Markets   (7, C2)

The glory days of Thailand's floating markets are over – but that's not to say you won't enjoy a leisurely morning boat trip to the markets on Khlong Damnoen Saduak and surrounding canals. Women in straw hats and blue shirts paddle their wooden boats laden with fresh fruit, vegetables and flowers. As the canals are a few hours away and you need to arrive early (around 8am), we suggest you take a tour but find one that lets you explore the most interesting markets, on Khlongs Damnoen Saduak and Khun Phitak. Avoid the unashamedly made-for-tourists Khlong Hia Kui like the plague.

Ko Kret   (1, B1)

This island in the middle of the Mae Nam Chao Phraya is a crafty little getaway in every sense. Known for its distinctive pottery, Ko Kret is visited by relatively few people, although it's just an hour away from the big smoke. It's a laidback place and home to one of Thailand's oldest Mon settlements. The Mon people, originally from Burma, are skilled potters, as the fine pieces in the small **Ancient Mon Pottery Centre** show. You can easily walk around Ko Kret in a few hours, stopping at pottery shops, which are usually underneath the artisans' stilted houses.

A crafty way to earn a living

Fine pottery for sale, Ko Kret

Muang Boran   (7, C4)

In the wrong hands, Muang Boran (Ancient City) could have been the Eurodisney of Thailand. But fortunately this enormous open-air museum was shaped by a philanthropist passionate about conserving Thailand's art and architectural traditions. It's such a genuinely wholesome place – all lush gardens, grazing wildlife, gushing streams and artisans at work – with so few visitors that you feel like you've stumbled onto a Thai *Sound of Music* set. More than 100 mini-replicas of important Thai buildings – from temples to traditional houses – and monuments are spread over the 128ha site in the shape of Thailand. You could easily spend a day walking or, better, riding a bike (50B) around. If you

INFORMATION

33km southeast of Bangkok
- 🚌 air-con 11 to Samat Prakan, then sawngtháew 36
- ✉ KM 33, old Th Sukhumvit
- ☎ 02 323 9253
- e www.ancientcity.com
- ⏰ 8am-5pm
- $ 50/25B adult/child
- 🍴 restaurant at the floating market

know your enthusiasm will wane after a few hours of heat, dust and humidity, you might want to plot your journey and target your must-sees on the free map – if you've already been to the Grand Palace, you probably won't get much out of seeing its replica, except for an appreciation of the artisans' skills. For a view of the entire site, climb the only hill (artificial, of course) topped by a copy of **Khao Phra Wihan**, a Khmer temple which sits atop an escarpment just over the border in Cambodia. The **Folk Museum** and its collection of traditional implements is worth a poke around to see how Thais once harvested their crops, wove cloth and managed their livestock. You won't want for shady pitstops, as there are plenty of cafes and restaurants, including the lovely teak restaurants at the floating markets.

Now that's what you call a couch – part of the open-air Muang Boran museum complex

ORGANISED TOURS

Be careful of bogus tour operators – only book tours through travel agencies or operators with official licenses from the Tourism Authority of Thailand.

Amazing Bangkok Cyclists (4, E5)
These popular trips start at the Imperial Tara Hotel and head to Prakanong, in the southeast, where you can ride freely and easily among fields and stilted houses.
✉ **Imperial Tara Hotel, Soi 26, Th Sukhumvit**
☎ **02 322 9481**
🕐 1pm-6pm ⑤ 750B

Manohra Rice Barge Dinner Cruise (1, H1)
Dinner cruises in Bangkok are a dime a dozen, but this is one in a million – a restored rice barge, stunning food and the riverside temples lit up at night.
✉ **Bangkok Marriott Resort & Spa, 257 Th**

There's more to dinner than rice on this restored barge.

Charoen Nakhon, Thonburi ☎ **02 476 0022** 🕐 7.30-10.30pm ⑤ from 1200B

Oriental Hotel's Cruise to Ayuthaya (2, P9) Fans of this luxurious tour to Ayuthaya recommend you book to travel there by coach and return by boat, so you can lunch as you float home.
✉ **Oriental Hotel, Soi Oriental, Th Charoen Krung, Bangrak** ☎ **02 859 9000** 🕐 8am-5pm ⑤ **1900B including lunch**

Thonburi Bike Tour (6, C1) Discover little-explored Thonburi – its orchards, lush gardens, canals, temples and floating markets – by bike on this ride organised by the Bangkok Tourist Bureau.
✉ **Bangkok Tourist Bureau, 17/1 Th Phra Athit, Banglamphu** ☎ **02 225 7612-4** 🕐 **1st Sun of the month, 9.30am-4pm** ⑤ **650B**

DIY Boat Tours

Escape the craziness by hiring a longtail to take you far, far away – you'll get a cool breeze, a change of scenery and get to see how the other thousands of Bangkok residents live.

The Thonburi canals are close and convenient for longtail journeys. One of the best trips is along Khlong Bangkok Noi, which gradually changes from a congested city canal to a route lined with greenery, houses on stilts and Wat Suwannaram, with exquisite *jakata* murals. Scenic Khlong Bangkok Yai travels past Wat Intharam, while Khlong Mon passes orchid farms.

The best places for hiring boats are **Tha Chang** (2, G2), **Tha Si Phraya** (2, O9) and **Tha Saphan Phut** (2, L4), where the going rate is around 400B an hour. Beware of agents who'll try to act as a broker between you and the boat driver (and scoop a nice commission) and make sure you establish a price before you get on the boat. If you don't want to barter, rent a longtail for 500B an hour through the riverside boat office, in front of **River City** (2, N9).

shopping

Even avowed anti-consumerism types weaken in Bangkok. One minute they're touting the virtues of a life without material possessions, the next they're admiring the fake Rolex on their wrist and finding out which Skytrain goes to Chatuchak.

If you intend launching a full-scale shopping assault, don't deny yourself a copy of the Nancy Chandler illustrated map of Bangkok; its garish 70s style may seem quaint and dated, but its information and insights are indispensable.

Shopping Areas

Serious shoppers usually start with a trawl of the strip of Th Phra Ram I from Siam Square (3, C7) to the corner of Th Ratchadamri (3, C9). This boulevard of retail bliss is the home of the heavyweight shopping centres, like **Mahboonkrong**, **Siam Centre** and **World Trade Centre**. Then when their thoughts turn to Thai arts, crafts and antiques, they head down to the river and the rarified air of River City (3, G2). Between here and the Oriental Hotel (3, J2), Th Charoen Krung and its offshoots boast craft shops. The sois off Th Sukhumvit (3 & 4) are also worth checking out for little outlets of fabric, antiques, celadon and other craftworks, not to mention the Emporium shopping centre.

But the highlight for most shoppers are the markets, loud and crazy places where you can buy anything and everything. If it's not at the rambling, claustrophobic **Chatuchak Weekend Market** (1, E3), then you can't get it in Bangkok. To live like a local, elbow your way through the produce and product markets of **Chinatown** (2, J6) and **Phahurat** (2, K4 & 2, J5). The best tourist markets – for that de rigueur fake handbag, watch or Western-sized clothing – are at **Patpong** (3, G7), **Sukhumvit** (3, D13) and **Banglamphu** (6, C4).

Bicycles, Buddha and flowers

DEPARTMENT STORES

Bangkok's department stores just don't have the sparkle or excitement of a Saks or Harvey Nics, but their sales are good enough to get the adrenalin pumping. Jocks despairing at the unsportiness of Bangkokians will find kindred spirits in the well-stocked sports departments.

Central (3, C10)
Central's flagship store is Bangkok's flashiest department store, complete with the requisite doormen and oh-so-subtle piano player. Ignore the clothes and head for the drool-worthy homewares floor, where you nose around teak furniture, celadon dinnersets and funky cutlery. Take a detour home via the sports department, with basketball net and skate ramp, and the Greyhound Cafe. Also at Silom Complex (3, G8).
✉ **1027 Th Ploenchit, Pratunam** ☎ **02 233 6930-9** 🚇 **Chitlom** 🚌 **air-con 1, 8, 11, 13** ⏰ **10am-9pm**

Robinson (3, G8)
Here's to you, good old Robinson, one of Bangkok's old faithful stores. It doesn't even try to offer the shopping experience of a lifetime, but is uncannily handy when you need a bottle of wine, some underwear and a

Shopping, Zen-style

new umbrella. Also at Th Sukhumvit, between Sois 17 and 19, and Th Charoen Krung, between sois 44 and 46.
✉ **2 Th Silom, Silom** 🚇 **Sala Daeng** 🚌 **air-con 2, 4, 5, 15** ⏰ **10.30am-9pm**

Sogo (3, C10)
Ever since it nabbed the Thai Craft Museum Shop from the in-renovation Gaysorn Plaza, this Japanese department store has suddenly become more appealing. Apart from that emporium, Sogo boasts some exclusive European designer accessories and shoes, a good supermarket and an antique shop with exquisite sandstone sculptures and hill-tribe jewellery.
✉ **494 Th Ploenchit, Pathumwan** ☎ **02 250 0017** 🚇 **Chitlom** 🚌 **air-con 1, 8, 11, 13** ⏰ **10am-10pm**

Zen (3, C9)
Zen sounds like the ultimate Asian minimalist designer store. But it's a branch of a Japanese department store, with nary a quietly bubbling fountain to help you reach pure shopping enlightenment. This busy store has a young focus – the clothing lines are pretty similar to Central's and it stocks Japanese brands like Shu Uemura and Shiseido.
✉ **World Trade Centre, cnr Th Phra Ram I & Th Ratchadamri, Pratunam** ☎ **02 255 9669** 🚇 **Chitlom** 🚌 **air-con 4, 5, 11, 13, 15** 🚤 **canal taxi to Nailert** ⏰ **10am-9pm**

SHOPPING CENTRES

Bangkok mall-rats have it good now that shopping centres have replaced parks as the public space of choice in this city starved of greenery and fresh air. There are loads of these mega-temples to consumerism – some even have bowling alleys, ice-skating rinks and fun-fairs.

The Emporium (4, D4)
The Emporium is the newest, too-cool-for-school shopping centre for urbanites with cash to splash. This Sukhumvit centre cleverly manages to cater for young urban princesses and stately establishment queens with the hippest fashion designers (Miu Miu, Prada), hardcore luxury brands (Chanel, Rolex) and classy eateries (Greyhound Café, Salon de l'Oriental) to see and be seen. And somehow it manages not to be intimidating.
✉ **btw Sois 22 & 24, Th Sumhumvit**
☎ **02 664 8000**
🚇 **Phrom Phong**
🚌 **air-con 1, 2, 8, 11, 13, 38** ⏰ **Mon-Fri 10.30am-10pm, Sat & Sun 10am-10pm**

Mahboonkrong
(3, C6) As one local put it, tourists get their fakes at the Patpong market, Thais get theirs at MBK. Its seemingly endless floors of stalls and shops, connected by streams of escalators, cater for the cheap and cheerful market, whether it's street fashion (if you fit Thai sizes), mobile phones, good fake watches or jewellery.
✉ **cnr Th Phra Ram I & Th Phayathai, Siam Sq** 🚇 **National Stadium** 🚌 **air-con 1, 2, 29, 141** ⏰ **10am-10pm**

Peninsula Plaza
(3, D9) Almost eerily quiet, bar the clicking of heels and an occasionally tinkling piano, the Peninsula Plaza is the most posh of Bangkok shopping centres. It's the turf of the serious, luxury-brand heavyweights who have no time for the hottest young designers du jour and just need their Louis Vuitton, Gianni Versace et al.
✉ **153 Th Ratchadamri**
🚇 **Ratchadamri**
🚌 **air-con 4, 5, 15**
⏰ **10am-10pm**

Panthip Plaza (3, A8)
Five floors of tech-head paradise, Panthip Plaza is dedicated to all things technical and technological – from mobile phones to pirated software (curiously, the 'real' technology companies don't seem to mind selling their product alongside the rip-off merchants).
✉ **Th Phetburi, Pratunam** 🚌 **air-con 5, 11, 12** ⛴ **river taxi to Nailert** ⏰ **10am-8pm**

River City (3, G2)
Only got time to visit one antiques place? Make a beeline for River City.

Reflections of life, Mahboonkrong facade

Everything sold in this four-floor complex of art, antiques and auctioneers is the very best, whether it's a Burmese Buddha image, the finest black silk or a benjarong teaset, and you pay for the quality. The stores can arrange to ship your buys back home.

✉ Th Yotha, Bangrak
☎ 02 237 0077
🚌 16, 36, 93
🚣 Tha Si Phraya
🕐 10am-10pm

Siam Centre & Siam Discovery Centre

(3, B7) If you've got a brand you want to flog to young, label-loving Thais, make sure you get a outlet at these Siam Square centres, linked by a walkway. Donna Karan, Kookai, Mambo and Bang &

Shrine outside the World Trade Centre

Olufsen did. So did UK homewares pioneer Habitat (trying for a brand reinvention, hey?).

✉ cnr Th Phayathai & Th Phra Ram 1 ☎ 02 658 1000-19 🚌 Siam

🚌 16, 21, 25, 40, 141
🕐 10am-9pm

World Trade Centre

(3, B9) What a difference a few years make. At the start of this century, the World Trade Centre wasn't tainted by history and was simply known as a monolithic shopping centre from which it was impossible to escape. That reputation stands for two reasons: shopaholics become all-consumed by the sheer number of fashion stores and anti-shopping types simply get lost.

✉ cnr Th Phra Ram I & Th Ratchadamri, Pratunam ☎ 02 255 9500
🚇 Chitlom 🚌 air-con 4, 5, 11, 13, 15
🚣 canal taxi to Nailert
🕐 10am-9pm

MARKETS

Amulet Market **(2, F6)**

Thais wear amulets for protection, usually from evil spirits or bad fortune. Wat Ratchanadta's market is one of the most famous places in Bangkok to buy amulets, which are usually of Buddha images but often Hindu deities, Thai monks and even phalluses, to protect against infertility.

✉ Wat Ratchanadta, cnr Ratchadamnoen Klang & Th Mahachai
🚌 air-con 5
🕐 9am-5pm

Banglamphu Market

(6, C4) The traders here know their market so well — you've got the hair-braiders, the henna tattoos, the bootleg CD-makers, the hippy jewellery stalls, the fake Birkenstocks, the 10B pad thai noodle-sellers, not

Fabric, hi-fi equipment, shirts – all that and much more at labyrinthine Phahurat Market

to mention an excellent range of clothes in big sizes. It's fun, lively and good value.

✉ **Th Chakraphong & Th Phra Sumen, Banglamphu**
🚌 air-con 6, 17
⛴ Tha Banglamphu
🕐 5-11pm

Nakhon Kasem (2, J6)

Nakhon Kasem, or Thieves Market, dates from Chinatown's seedier days when it was a dumping ground for stolen goods. But today it's a seemingly respectable place with some good shops selling art and antiques, musical instruments and other odds and sods.

✉ **Th Charoen Krung, Chinatown**
🚌 air-con No 1, 7, 8
⛴ Tha Ratchawong
🕐 10am-8pm

Pak Khlong Market (2, K4)

Get up early or stay out late to catch this 24hr market at its most raucous, as the city stocks up on its orchids, lilies and other tropical flowers. Pak Khlong is Bangkok's biggest and most famous flower market, though it has some good fruit and vegie stalls.

✉ **Th Chakraphet, near Tha Ratchini, Phahurat**
🚌 air-con 6 ⛴ Tha Ratchini 🕐 24hrs

Patpong Night Market (3, H5)

Crammed with 'real, genuine fakes', Patpong is the most popular, but not cheapest, tourist market. With one eye on the goods and the other on girls gyrating around poles close by, shoppers jostle past each other to buy every-

Driving a Hard Bargain

Thais respect a good bargainer, someone who can get a reasonable price without either seller or buyer losing face. Here are some hints:

- do your homework on prices
- don't start bargaining unless you intend to buy
- always let the vendor make the first offer and then ask 'is that your best price?'
- don't be aggressive or raise your voice; be friendly
- remember that there's a fine line between bargaining and niggling – how much is 10B really worth to you, anyway?

Happiness is a good sales day, Pak Khlong Market.

thing from fake Mooks T-shirts to Osama bin Laden masks. Have a clear mind about what you want to pay before you begin bargaining.

✉ **Sois 1 & 2, Th Silom, Patpong** 🚈 Sala Daeng 🚌 air-con 2, 4, 5, 15 🕐 2pm-2am

Phahurat Market (2, J5)

If your sense of direction is shocking, enter

Try faking it at Patpong Night Market.

this warren of shops selling fabrics, haberdashery, Indian jewellery, samosas and saris at your peril. After a while, every little laneway within Little India's famous, labyrinthine market begins to look the same. But persevere as you'll uncover some incredible bargains on your journey.

✉ **Th Phahurat, Phahurat** 🚌 1, 3, 5, 7, 8, 21, 25, 37, 40, 48, 56 🚇 Tha Saphan Phut ⏰ 10am-9pm

Pratunam Market

(3, A9) Pratunam market is where the city's African community goes to shop. Like Chatuchak it sells a bit of everything, but you can uncover some clothing gems, whether you're after a Hawaiian shirt, Cookie Monster slippers or knee-high silver boots with tassles.

✉ **Th Phetburi, Pratunam** 🚌 air-con 4, 13, 15, 38, 139, 140 🚇 canal taxi to Nailert ⏰ 10am-10pm

Sampeng Market

(2, K7) You can get anything you want in Sampeng Lane, or Soi Wanit 1, as long as you appreciate the concept of economies of scale. Thongs? Take a 12-pack. An inflatable Superman? They've got five for 400B. If you look hard,

Flowers for sale, Pak Khlong Market

you'll find some shopfronts selling tea and tobacco, just like in the old days.

✉ **Soi Wanit (Sampeng La), Chinatown** 🚌 air-con 8 🚇 Tha Ratchawong ⏰ 10am-10pm

Soi Lalai Sap Market

(3, H6) Literally 'the soi that melts your money away', this street is jampacked at lunchtime with Thai workers bargaining for fake handbags and other leathergoods, homewares and clothing. It's just next to the Bangkok Bank on Th Silom.

✉ **Soi 5, Th Silom** 🚇 Sala Daeng 🚌 air-con 2, 4, 5, 15 ⏰ Mon-Fri 10am-3pm

Sukhumvit Market

(3, D13) A market for the true fake aficionado, who knows the seriously big difference between a good faux Fendi handbag and one with dodgy stitching and a bum zip. Other top imitations include: soccer kits (Becks, Giggsy and Zidane dominate), watches, sunglasses, Levis and jewellery. The wooden travel games, like Chinese chequers and backgammon, are originals and look fun.

✉ **btw Sois 2 & 12, 3 & 15, Th Sukhumvit, Khlong Toey** 🚇 Nana 🚌 air-con 1, 8, 11, 13 ⏰ 11am-10.30pm

Thewet Flower Market (2, B6)

Unless you're a local, most of Thewet market is for looking rather than buying, though a bunch of purple orchids or some jasmine garlands can jazz up your hotel room no end. This garden market, known for its cheap prices and its stalls of tropical plants, lines the northern bank of Khlong Phadung Krung Kasem.

✉ **Th Krung Kasem, Dusit** 🚌 air-con No 3, 6, 17 🚇 Tha Thewet

---

For Good Measure

Nothings fits? If you're not Thai-sized but are determined to return with a *très* tropical wardrobe, your best bet is to get clothes made by a tailor (bring fabric with you or, even better, pick up some silk here) or to shop at the tourist markets, such as Banglamphu, which cater for comparatively hefty Westerners.

JEWELLERY & SILVERWARE

As one of the world's biggest exporters of gems and ornaments, Thailand offers some good buys in unset gems, especially jade, rubies and sapphires, and finished jewellery – but that's if you know what you're doing. If you can't tell blue glass from a sapphire, buy from reputable dealers. The shops we list have been recommended by expats.

Johnny's Gems (2, J5)
Johnny's is consistently recommended as a reliable jeweller. Expats keep going back again and again for the set jewellery and attentive service.
✉ **199 Th Fuang Nakhon, off Th Charoen Krung, Phra Nakhon** ☎ **02 222 1756** 🚌 **air-con 1, 7, 8** 🚢 **Tha Tien** ⏰ **10am-7pm**

Lin Jewellers (2, P9)
Lin might be a bit pricier than your average Bangkok silver shop but you know you're getting the genuine article. You can pick up some classic pieces, like silver chokers, thick bangles and delicate chains.
✉ **9 Soi 38, Th Charoen Krung, Bangrak** ☎ **02 234 2819** 🚢 **Saphan Taksin** 🚢 **Tha Oriental** 🚌 **75, 115, 116** ⏰ **10am-8pm**

Lin Silvercraft (2, P9)
The sister shop of Lin Jewellers around the corner, this silverware shop is crammed to the rafters with quality knick-knacks and tableware, including a sugar bowl with a handleless milk jug that moulds into the shape of your hand.
✉ **14 Soi Oriental, Th Charoen Krung, Bangrak** ☎ **02 235 2108** 🚢 **Saphan Taksin** 🚌 **75, 115, 116** 🚢 **Tha Oriental** ⏰ **10am-8pm**

SV Jewellery (2, P9)
With a big showroom on bustling Th Charoen Krung, SV Jewellery isn't just a shop for girly baubles and body decoration. You'll find cufflinks in all sizes, shapes and attitudes, silver animals (including especially cute elephants) and homewares, like enormous gleaming photoframes and keyrings.
✉ **1254-6 Th Charoen Krung, Bangrak** ☎ **02 233 7347** 🚢 **Saphan**

Taksin 🚢 **Tha Oriental** 🚌 **75, 115, 116** ⏰ **10am-8pm**

Uthai's Gems (3, E11)
You need to make an appointment to see Uthai's gems in quiet Soi Ruam Rudee. His fixed prices and good service make him a popular choice among expats.
✉ **28/7 Soi Ruam Rudi, Th Ploenchit** ☎ **02 253 8582** 🚇 **Ploenchit** 🚌 **air-con 1, 8, 11, 13**

All that Glitters
Ah, the gem scam. We all know of someone who's been duped but, still, it's so easy to be lulled into a false sense of security abroad. Let the warning bells ring when a friendly local approaches you and, after some chatter, casually asks you along to their friend's gem shop. The gem scam usually ends with you being talked into buying low-grade gems and posting them home, where you'll find out they're worth very little. Just remember that your average Thai doesn't just start talking to strange foreigners and a deal too good to be true almost certainly is.

CLOTHING

Jaspal (3, B9)

With a finger on the pulse of Western trends and a constant eye on the international fash mags, Jaspal is a home-grown, high-street label for guys and girls. Also at the Emporium and Siam Centre.

✉ 2nd fl, World Trade Centre, cnr Th Phra Ram I & Th Ratchadamri, Pratunam
☎ 02 255 9500
🚉 Chitlom 🚌 air-con 4, 5, 11, 13, 15
⛴ canal taxi to Nailert
🕐 10am-9pm

Greyhound (4, D4)

Greyhound makes sleek streetwear for urbanites. Like many fashion houses, it's expanding to become a lifestyle brand that includes its chain of minimalist Greyhound Cafes (see p. 81). You can pick up some basics with an edge, like pants, T-shirts and belts.

✉ 2nd fl, The Emporium, btw Sois 22 & 24 Th Sukhumvit
☎ 02 664 8664
🚉 Phrom Phong Skytrain 🕐 Mon-Fri 10.30am-10pm, Sat-Sun 10am-10pm

Shopping for clothes is no speedy pursuit at Greyhound.

TAILORS

Classic 88 (2, P9)

Classic 88 has an excellent selection of quality fabrics, especially silks, and comes with the blessing of many satisfied customers. As its name suggests, it's a good place for classic tailored clothing, like silk shirts, suits and shift dresses — nothing radical but very reliable. If you forget something, just place an order through its website.

✉ 1340-2 Th Charoen Krung, Bangrak ☎ 02 233 0149 @ www.class ic-88.com 🚌 Saphan Taksin 🚌 75, 115, 116
⛴ Tha Sathorn
🕐 10am-6pm

Miss Hong (3, C13)

The highly recommended Miss Hong has been making women and children's clothes for years and is known for her attention to detail. Call to make an appointment to see her in her studio in the heart of Little Arabia. It's a good idea to take along a picture to show what look and style you're after.

✉ 6/25-6 Soi 3, Th Sukhumvit ☎ 02 253 5662 🚌 Nana
🚌 air-con 1, 8 , 11, 13

Raja's Fashions

(3, D13) Raja's thrives on a top-notch reputation for men's tailoring (it seems to have besuited Bangkok's

Suit Yourself

It's tough going back to that off-the-rack circus once you've had a suit made by a good tailor. But to get the best out of bespoke, keep this in mind:

- look for quality workmanship and always insist on at least two fittings for a suit.
- don't go for deals offering one suit, two shirts, three ties, with an extra safari suit thrown in, for US$100 – the product will be too bad to be true.
- bring a magazine picture to show what you want. You may fancy yourself as a George Clooney-type but they might be thinking Bill Gates.

entire US expat population) and snappy slogans. Just wait for Raja to tell you, like every one of your predecessors, when you have your final suit fitting, 'You came in good looking and now you're looking good'. Why change a winning formula?
✉ **1/6 Soi 4, Th Sumhumvit** ☎ 02 253 8379 🚇 Nana
🚌 air-con 1, 8, 11, 13
🕐 Mon-Sat 10.30am-8pm

THAI SILK

Jim Thompson (3, G7)
As you'd expect of the company that single-handedly resurrected the Thai silk industry, you get nothing but impeccable-quality fabric at Jim Thompson, though you do pay for the brand. You can buy silk by the metre, ready-made into clothing and accessories or get yourself an outfit whipped up by the in-house tailors.
✉ **9 Th Suriwong, Silom (also at World Trade Centre, the Emporium & Central Chidlom)** ☎ 02 632 8100 🚇 Sala Daeng
🚌 1, 16, 35, 36, 75, 93
🕐 9am-9pm

Lea Silk (3, B11)
Dutch-born textile artist Lea Dingjan-Laarakker employs hundreds of Isan women to weave the high-quality silk that she uses as a canvas for her striking modern designs. Almost all the profits she makes from sales are invested into community development programs for Isan villages. Call her for an appointment at her studio at the Hilton to see her original art.
✉ **Promenade Arcade,**

The Real Deal

The big-name international designers heavily discount their stock during sales, so you might nab a good bargain, especially if your currency is fighting fit. (If not, there's always the Sukhumvit or Patpong markets, where we spied some well-heeled types buying up handbag rip-offs in Burberry tartan and Louis Vuitton graffiti.) See what's hot at these designer shops in the Emporium:

Chanel	☎ 02 664 8621-5
DKNY	☎ 02 664 8450-3
Fendi	☎ 02 664 8396-7
Gianni Versace	☎ 02 664 8387-9
Hermes	☎ 02 664 8353-4
Kenzo	☎ 02 664 8407-8
Louis Vuitton	☎ 02 664 8360-1
Miu Miu	☎ 02 664 8487-9
Prada	☎ 02 2664 8430-3

Hilton International Bangkok, 967 Th Phra Ram I ☎ 02 258 2332 🚇 Chitlom 🚌 air-con 1, 8, 11, 13

Shinawatra (4, A2)
Shinawatra's massive showroom may be tricky to find (take the first street on the right off Soi 23, then the first left) but you'll have a new-found respect for the industriousness of Thai silkworms when you arrive. Just how many of them did it take to create the fabric which Shinawatra dyes into every possible hue or makes up into clothes, accessories and tablewares?
✉ **94 Soi 23, Th Sukhumvit** ☎ 02 258 0295-9 🚇 Asok
🚌 air-con 1, 2, 8, 11, 13, 38 🕐 Mon-Sat 8.30am-5.30pm

ARTS & CRAFTS

Look out for celadon (green-glazed porcelain) and benjarong (five-colour porcelain) pieces, blue-and-white china, wickerware, hand-beaten silverware and bronzeware, woven cottons and silks, nielloware (silver inlaid with niello) and khon masks.

CERAMIC WARE

Damrongluck Benjarong (3, G2)

By itself, each benjarong porcelain piece is delicate but put hundreds together in a shop and you get a big glaring eyeful. This benjarong shop, situated in the River City complex, uses 10 core designs to create its teasets, vases, covered bowls and dining settings, which can be made to order and shipped almost anywhere in the world.

⌧ 3rd fl, River City, Th Yotha ☎ 02 639 0716 ⎚ 16, 36, 93 ⚓ Tha Si Phraya ⏲ 10am-10pm

EMPORIUMS

Narai Phand (3, B9)

As a government-run, not-for-profit enterprise for distributing handicrafts made by Thai villagers, Narai Phand has its heart in the right place. Though no matter how often you

remind yourself of this, this multilevel warehouse still feels like a souvenir factory. (But you won't worry about that when you dash in to buy a celadon teacup for Auntie Doris 10mins before you leave for the airport.)

⌧ 127 Th Ratchadamri, Siam Sq ☎ 02 252 4670 ⚓ Chitlom ⚓ canal taxi to Nailert ⎚ air-con 4, 5, 11, 13, 15 ⏲ 10am-9pm

Silom Village (3, H4)

It's blissfully easy to wander around this cluster of shops in wooden buildings. Some vendors sell the ubiquitous touristy fare while the antique shops have some eye-catching pieces from Thailand, Cambodia and Burma. With a pitstop at the casual restaurant, you could spend a few hours here, no problems.

⌧ 286 Th Silom, Silom

⚓ Chong Nonsi ⎚ air-con 2, 4, 5, 15 ⏲ 10am-9pm

Exotique Thai (4, D4)

Have a good squizz around the shelves and hanging racks of this emporium and you'll find some everyday Thai craftworks and home-wares with a contemporary twist, including lines by up-and-coming designer homebrands like Fai Sor Kam. Fans of Asian-inspired fashion will have a field day trying on the luxurious sarongs or picking out groovy silk ties.

⌧ 4th fl, The Emporium, btw Sois 22 & 24, Th Sukhumvit ☎ 02 664 8000 ex 1554 ⚓ Phrom Phong ⎚ air-con 1, 2, 8, 11, 13, 38 ⏲ Mon-Fri 10.30am-10pm, Sat-Sun 10am-10pm

Chitlada Shop (2, B10)

This is probably as close as you'll get to the royal family – so remember to dress respectfully (girls, wear long skirts and closed shoes). The Chitlada Shop, at the palace where the king and queen live, is an outlet of the nonprofit Support organisation which promotes the practice of traditional craft-making skills, so everything is authentic.

⌧ Chitlada Palace, Dusit ☎ 02 282 8435 ⎚ air-con 9, 10, 16, 18, 24, 92 ⏲ 10am-4.30pm

Ko Kret it, Pottery Buffs

Ko Kret (see p. 54) is one big pottery shop. It's the home of the local Mon people who make unique terracotta pottery.

Thai Craft Museum Shop (3, C10)

Don't ask us why it's called a museum shop. We only know it as one of the best one-stop Thai craft shops, where collections of celadon, traditional woven cottons, nielloware, wood carvings and basketry are within a few steps of each other. It's settling comfortably into its new home after moving across the road from Gaysorn Plaza.

✉ 4th fl, Erawan Sogo, 494 Th Ploenchit, Pathumwan ☎ 02 250 0017 🚇 Chitlom 🚌 air-con 1, 8, 11, 13 🕐 10am-10pm

Krishna's (3, D14)

Krishna's is a treasure-trove of Asiana in all sizes and styles, from a tiny benjarong plate to Nepalese prints to a coffee table which balances on a bronze bear's paws. It can arrange to send your purchases home.

✉ btw Sois 9 & 11, Th Sukhumvit ☎ 02 253 7693 🚇 Nana 🚌 air-con 1, 8, 11, 13 🕐 Mon-Sat 9am-10pm

Rasi Sayam (4, A2)

Rasi Sayam is all class. Based in a Thai house, it sells delicate woven wall-hangings and the most intricately created baskets, as well as pottery and sandstone statues.

✉ 32 Soi 23, Th Sukhumvit ☎ 02 258 4195 🚇 Asok 🚌 air-con 1, 2, 8, 11, 13, 38 🕐 Mon-Sat 9am-5.30pm

Thai Home Industries

(2, P9) You can wander at will around this enormous traditional Thai building

Just a few million Buddha images for sale

overflowing with boxes and packaging. The staff tend to leave you to your own devices to poke around the wooden cabinets displaying bronzeware, silverware (especially cutlery) and basketry. Keep an eye out for the great temple bells.

✉ 35 Soi Oriental, Th Charoen Krung, Bangrak ☎ 02 234 1736 🚇 Saphan Taksin 🚢 Tha Oriental & hotel shuttle boat from Tha Sathorn 🚌 75, 115, 116 🕐 10am-8pm

SPECIALITY SHOPS

Nadakwang (4, A3)

There's a comforting, down-home feel about Nadakwang, from the cosy wooden shopfront right down to its smallest woven drinks coaster. Expats have long loved this shop's top-quality tableware, stocking up on good-value embroidered cotton napkins and tablecloths. To get there, take the first street on the right as you head north up Soi 23.

✉ 108/3 Soi 23, Th Sukhumvit ☎ 02 258 1962 🚇 Nana

🚌 air-con 1, 2, 8, 11, 13, 38 🕐 Mon-Sat 9am-5pm, Sun 10am-5pm

Siam Bronze Factory

(2, P9) We know it's crass to rave on about bargains, but we can't hold back about Siam Bronze. The quality of its hand-beaten brassware and silverware is astonishing, even more so when you compare its prices to other outlets. Don't dare buy bronzeware anywhere else.

✉ 1250 Th Charoen Krung, Bangrak ☎ 02 234 9436 🚇 Saphan Taksin 🚌 75, 115, 116 🚢 Tha Oriental 🕐 10am-7pm

Celadon House

(2, E14) A house of celadon indeed it is – with celadon in many colours (green, blue and brown), shapes and sizes. Make sure you check out the seconds room out the back where some pieces are heavily reduced.

✉ 8/6-8 Soi Rajadapisek (Soi 16), Th Sukhumvit ☎ 02 259 7744 🚇 Asok 🚌 air-con 22, 38, 136 🕐 10am-7pm

ANTIQUES

Nagi Shop (3, E15)
This dark little shop at the Siam Society has a curious collection of pieces from throughout Thailand, including hill-tribe jewellery, and Cambodia. You might find some gems among the antique books, including some amusing travelogues of Siamese adventures, maps and lithographs.
✉ 131 Soi 21 (Soi Asoke), Th Sukhumvit
☎ 02 661 6480
🚇 Asok 🚌 air-con 22, 38, 136 ⏰ Tues-Sat 9am-5pm

l'Arcadia (4, B2)
The buyer at l'Arcadia has a sharp eye for collectibles from Burma, Cambodia and Thailand, including Sukhothai cabinets, cute red-lacquer containers, Khmer-style sandstone figures and carved, wooden temple decorations. If you simply can't resist that Burmese lounge chair, the

l'Arcadia's collection of Khmer-style collectibles

shop can arrange to have it shipped home.
✉ 12/2 Soi 23, Th Sukhumvit ☎ 02 259 9595 🚇 Asok
🚌 air-con 1, 2, 8, 11, 13, 38 ⏰ 9am-10pm

Charlie's Collection (3, G2) Charlie's a bit of a character – and a good thing, too. Otherwise his eccentric shop of antiques and collectibles – including fabulous coloured-glass, Art Deco lamps and Thai royal family (dare we say) kitsch – wouldn't be half as much fun. And there's not much of that in serious old River City.
✉ 4th fl, River City, Th Yotha, Bangrak ☎ 02 237 0077 🚌 16, 36, 93 ⛴ Tha Si Phraya ⏰ 10am-10pm

Old Maps & Prints (3, G2) You could poke around in this shop for hours, flipping through the maps of Siam and Indochina, laughing at early explorers' quaint drawings of 'the natives' and simply sighing with delight at the framed prints that are out of your price range.
✉ 4th fl, River City, Th Yotha, Bangrak ☎ 02 237 0077-8 🚌 No 16, 36, 93 ⛴ Tha Si Phraya ⏰ 11am-7pm

Prasart Collection (3, C9) Run by Prasart Vongsakul, of the highly regarded Prasart Museum east of Bangkok, this shop is the Rolls Royce of antique collections. His excellent range of chinaware – including delicate blue-and-white pieces as well as benjarong – and Buddha images are just too tempting for your own good.
✉ 2nd fl, Peninsula Plaza, 153 Th Ratchadamri, Lumphini ☎ 02 253 9772 🚇 Ratchadamri 🚌 air-con 4, 5, 15 ⏰ 10am-10pm

Love Hurts
Be careful before you start falling in love with statues or images of Buddhas and other deities. It can be an administrative nightmare taking them home – you need a licence from the Department of Fine Arts and a permit from the Ministry of Commerce (though you can take out the small Buddha images meant to be worn around your neck). If you want to take an antique home, you need to apply for a licence from Fine Arts. Contact the National Museum on ☎ 02 226 1661 for more information.

MUSIC & BOOKS

You won't go without books in Bangkok but pop-hating music fans might feel a bit limited by the music stores. Many head to Banglamphu, where a highly illegal, pirated CD goes for around 100B.

Asia Books (3, D14)
You can't beat Asia Books for its sheer breadth of English-language books, nor for its attentive service. The book chain-cum-empire has the best and biggest selection of books on Asia in Bangkok. Other stores include: at the Emporium, Landmark Plaza, Peninsula Plaza, Thaniya Plaza and World Trade Centre.
✉ 221 Th Sukhumvit (at Soi 15) ☎ 02 252 7277 🚇 Asok 🚌 air-con 1, 8 , 11, 13 ⏰ 9am-9pm

Bookazine (3, C7)
For a magazine fix, head to Bookazine, which imports an excellent range of glossies from around the world in many languages, as well as the major newspapers. Its English-language book selection isn't bad and it sells some foreign-language literature.
✉ 286 Siam Sq ☎ 02 255 3778 🚇 Siam 🚌 16, 21, 25, 40, 141 ⏰ 10am-10pm

CD Warehouse (3, C7)
If you can bear the Asia-pop that reverberates throughout these vast stores, a visit could easily stretch into the hours. Its catalogue is dominated by mainstream tastes, but you can usually find something that takes your fancy, even if it's not *the* one you were after. If you love Enrique Iglesias and Britney Spears,

you'll be in clover.
✉ L4, Siam Centre, Siam Sq 🚇 Siam 🚌 16, 21, 25, 40, 141 ⏰ 10am-9pm

Merman Books (3, G8)
Asiana aficionados won't be able to pull themselves away. Run by a former *Bangkok Post* editor, Merman Books specialises in out-of-print and rare titles on Asia, with shelves crammed with obscure sociology titles, a fair whack of

biographies and travel-nerd collectibles like 1st editions of legendary guidebooks.
✉ 2nd fl, Silom Complex, 191 Th Silom ☎ 02 2231 3155 🚇 Sala Daemg Sky-train ⏰ 10.30am-8.30pm

Shaman Books (6, D4)
As you'd expect, well-thumbed Jack Kerouac paperbacks are in abundance. There's also an exciting selection of Asian travel literature and nonfiction. Shaman is not the cheapest second-hand bookshop around but it's certainly one of the best organised (everything is catalogued by computer) and has enough varieties of trashlit and brainfood to keep everyone suitably amused.
✉ 71 Th Khao San, Banglamphu ☎ 02 251 1467 🚌 air-con 6, 17 ⚓ Tha Banglamphu ⏰ 10am-10pm

Bangkok in Print

Unfortunately, the two genres dominating most recent English-language fiction on Bangkok are the 'middle-aged expat escapade' or 'zany college student chucks in the good life for life-defying adventures in crazy Bangkok'. Some better reads are:

- the intriguing *Hello My Big Big Honey!: Love Letters to Bangkok Bar Girls and Their Revealing Interviews*, edited by Dave Walker & Richard S Ehrlich
- *Jasmine Nights*, a novel by prolific Thai renaissance man SP Somtow
- *Bangkok in Black & White*, an edgy coffee-table book by top Thai photographer Manit Sriwanichpoorn

FOOD & DRINK

Stock up on curry pastes, fish sauce, a bamboo steamer and pot to make sticky rice and a coconut grater for coconut milk. For its novelty value (not its taste), buy a bottle of Chateau de Loey, Thailand's first wine.

Emporium Supermarket (4, D4)

Shopping at the Emporium for your daily groceries is a bit like popping down to Harrods for some milk and a piece of fillet steak for dinner. It stocks an excellent line of gourmet items for expats and is the place where you might just find that toiletry item from home you can't live without.

✉ **5th fl, The Emporium, btw Sois 22 & 24, Th Sukhumvit** ☎ **02 664 8000** 🚇 **Phrom Phong** 🚌 **air-con 1, 2, 8, 11, 13, 38** ⏰ **Mon-Fri 10.30am-10pm, Sat & Sun 10am-10pm**

Foodland Supermarket (3, C13)

The best-located 24hr supermarket, Foodland is perfect for a late-night snack or last-minute water refuelling stop. Its noodle

Head downstairs to Tops.

bar, also open around the clock, must be the only place in Bangkok where you can get a beer at 5am these days.

✉ **btw Sois 3/1 & 5, Th Sukhumvit** ☎ **02 530 0220** 🚇 **Nana** 🚌 **air-con 1, 8, 11, 13** ⏰ **24hrs**

Tops Supermarket (3, G8)

You'll find these excellent Dutch-run supermarkets – which are handily open until late – in the Central and Robinson department stores. Even better are the Tops Marketplace stores which have excellent ranges of local and imported fruit, vegetables, smallgoods and meats, plus a liquor store.

✉ **Central, 2 Th Silom, Silom** ☎ **02 632 7525** 🚇 **Sala Daeng** 🚌 **air-con 2, 4, 5, 15** ⏰ **9am-midnight**

FOR CHILDREN

Big kids will be fighting for the animal-shaped kites sold at Chatuchak, Sanam Luang and Lumphini Park in kite-flying season. The tourist markets are great for kids – Banglamphu has a stall of Batman and Superman outfits and fairy costumes.

ABC Babyland (3, B9)
This is the MBK of kids' stores – nothing is particularly classy but everything is pretty good. It's a vast supermarket-style shop, meaning it's a good spot to stock up on cheap clothing, toys and essentials, like nappies.
✉ **2nd fl, World Trade Centre, cnr Th Phra Ram I & Th Ratchadamri, Pratunam**
☎ **02 255 9500**
🚇 **Chitlom** 🚤 **canal taxi to Nailert**
🚌 **air-con 4, 5, 11, 13, 15** ⏱ **10am-9pm**

Buy Buy Kido (3, E14)
This enormous showroom covers the baby experience from go to whoa, starting from a big range of maternity wear to consultants to help you design junior's bedroom to towers of toys (all part of the Buy Buy Kido range) that the kids will go nuts over.
✉ **4 Soi 12, Th Sukhumvit** ☎ **02 229 5855-8** 🚇 **Asok**

Detail of artwork on kite, Sanam Luang

🚌 **air-con 1, 8 , 11, 13**
⏱ **10am-6pm**

Motif & Maris (3, G2)
It's rare to find someone in the rag trade still dedicated to the old arts of embroidery and smocking, so Motif & Maris is a surprise. Every piece of children's clothing hanging in this little shop is intricate and

exquisite. The handmade soft toys and nursery accessories are pretty gorgeous, too.
✉ **River City, Th Yotha, Bangrak**
☎ **02 237 0077 ex 220**
🚌 **16, 36, 93**
🚤 **Tha Si Phraya**
⏱ **10am-10pm**

Pet Farm Workshop (4, D4) If you've got loads of patience, your little one should have a ball at this make-your-own-stuffed-toy shop. First they pick the toy's face and coat, then its stuffing and voice. Then it's off to the hairdresser to fluff up the coat before a quick trip to the stylist for an outfit. Swing by the registrar for the birth certificate and then the toy's all theirs.
✉ **3rd fl, Jamboree, The Emporium, btw Sois 22 & 24, Th Sukhumvit** ☎ **02 664 8000** 🚇 **Phrom Phong**
🚌 **air-con 1, 2, 8, 11, 13, 38** ⏱ **Mon-Fri 10.30am-10pm, Sat & Sun 10am-10pm**

Dolls for sale, Th Phra Athit

SPECIALIST STORES

Alta Moda (3, C9)
Silk doesn't take your fancy or, ahem, suit your tailoring needs? It might be worth your while dropping by Alta Moda before visiting your tailor. This shop imports reams and reams of fabric from international design houses like YSL. Its huge showroom is roll-to-roll with fabrics ranging from slippery satin to starchy linen to flowery cottons. Also at the Emporium.
✉ **1st fl, World Trade Centre, cnr Th Phra Ram I & Th Ratchadamri, Pratunam**
☎ **02 255 9500**
🚇 **Chitlom** ⛴ **canal taxi to Nailert**
🚌 **air-con 4, 5, 11, 13, 15** ⏰ **10am-9pm**

Propaganda (4, D4)
If Propaganda is truly trying to live up to its name, then count us as officially manipulated. It's hard to resist the charms of this fun, stark-white shop with all sorts of functional design pieces

Alta Moda, fabric city

created by Thai designers – like 'the shark' bottle opener, practical semi-circular plates and (Brett Whiteley fans take note) giant matchstick lamps.
✉ **4th fl, The Emporium, btw Sois 22 & 24, Th Sukhumvit**
☎ **02 664 8574**
🚇 **Phrom Phong**
🚌 **air-con 1, 2, 8, 11, 13, 38** ⏰ **Mon-Fri 10.30am-10pm, Sat & Sun 10am-10pm**

Shanghai Tang (4, D4)
Fans of Chinese kitsch will be quivering under their khaki-and-red-star caps with excitement at Shanghai Tang. It's absolutely packed with bright and funky wares such as Mao ashtrays, loud dressing gowns and funny T-shirts. Check out the cool range of kid's clothes.
✉ **1st fl, The Emporium, btw Sois 22 & 24, Th Sukhumvit**
☎ **02 664 8470**
🚇 **Phrom Phong**
🚌 **air-con 1, 2, 8, 11, 13, 38** ⏰ **Mon-Fri 10.30am-10pm, Sat & Sun 10am-10pm**

Lamps for sale and window display, Propaganda

places to eat

It's a rare moment when Bangkok residents aren't eating, planning their next meal or talking about food. They munch continually on small meals, eat out often (where they'll probably debate with friends and family about food) and at all hours of the day and night.

Traditionally, Bangkokians ate mostly Central Thai food. But a steadily increasing migrant population has helped Bangkok evolve into one of South-East Asia's most exciting food destinations. Northeastern Thais coming to Bangkok to seek their fortune brought their popular Isan dishes. The Europeans established upmarket French, Italian and German restaurants around Th Sukhumvit and Th Silom. Districts like Little Arabia, Little India and Chinatown are dynamic areas with authentic restaurants.

Meal Costs

The pricing symbols used in this chapter indicate the cost of a two-course meal for one person, including all taxes and charges, and excluding drinks.

$	under 99B
$$	100-349B
$$$	350-599B
$$$$	over 600B

Eating, Thai-style

Eating is a social occasion to be shared with as many people as possible. Everyone orders a certain type of dish – like curry, salad or soup – and takes a small amount from each. Soups are served in communal bowls – spoon the broth into your dish or help yourself from the bowl.

Thais eat with a spoon and a fork, using the fork to push food onto the spoon. To them, putting a fork in your mouth is the height of bad manners. It's okay to use your hands when eating sticky rice – roll the rice into a ball and eat it with your right hand. You'll only be offered chopsticks with Chinese meals.

Thais aren't fussy about eating certain dishes at certain times – they might have curry and rice for breakfast or perhaps red pork. Some dishes are designated as 'drinking food', like deep-fried chicken knuckles or spicy salads.

Drinks

Thanks to a hefty government tax, alcoholic drinks are comparatively expensive in Bangkok. And, most nigglingly, many top-end restaurants will only serve bottled water for a shocking sum like 160B.

Wine addicts should take a deep breath before reading a restaurant wine list – what you'd consider cheap plonk back home is likely to cost upwards of US$20. Most beer drinkers choose Singha, Kloster, Carlsberg or Beer Chang as their tipple.

THAI FOOD

Thai cuisine can be both delicate and explosive, sophisticated and simple. But even though it swings between such extremes, its secret ingredient is balance. To understand this, just look at a typical Thai dinner table. It will inevitably be laden with a curry dish, a salad, a stir-fry, a soup, vegetables and a fish dish – a broad range of flavours, with each dish unlike, but still complementing, the others. Diners add condiments to each of these dishes to change the balance between the four key flavours – chilli to adjust the heat, fish sauce for the saltiness, vinegar with chilli for the sourness and sugar for the sweetness. The only dish not to be tinkered with is the rice *(khâo)*, which is so crucial to Thai culture that *kin khâo* (literally 'to eat rice') is the phrase for eating. The second-most revered staple is the humble noodle.

Herbs, Spices & Chillis

Thai food would be nothing without the punch of its herbs and spices, not to mention the king hit of chilli. Thais have an emotional attachment to their chillis and you, too, may well get a bit teary after a few too many of the tiny bird's eye chillis which lurk in spicy salads and are Thailand's hottest. Thais don't add salt to their food, instead using fish sauce *(nàam plaa)* or shrimp paste for saltiness. Other key flavours come from coriander, basil (three varieties), lemon grass, ginger, galangal, garlic and shallots.

Regional Specialities

Thailand has four main food regions, though every little village within these areas has its own speciality. Thai food most eaten outside of Thailand – your green curry *(kaeng khiaw-wan)*, red curry *(kaeng phèt)* and chilli, prawn and lemon grass soup *(tòm yam kûng)* – is Central Thai cuisine, known for its strong flavours. Bangkokians, though part of Central Thailand, are particularly fond of the Isan food of Northeastern Thailand, where grilling and roasting predominates. Don't miss trying the famous minced-meat salad *(lâap)* or classic Isan dish of grilled chicken *(kài yâang)*, green papaya salad *(sôm-tam)* and sticky rice *(khâo nîaw)*. Sticky rice is also popular in Northern Thailand, which is known for its sausages and Burmese-style curries. Southern Thai dishes have Chinese, Muslim and Thai influences – probably best epitomised by a Muslim curry *(kaeng màtsàman)*.

BANGLAMPHU

To get to Banglamphu, take the express boat to Tha Banglamphu. Buses travel along Th Phra Athit (air-con No 6) and Th Khao San (air-con No 6, 17). Just about all these buses go via Democracy Monument, from where any of these places are a short walk away.

Arawy (2, F5) $
Thai vegetarian
Blink and you'll miss this vegetarian eatery, not only because it's small and inconspicuous, but also because its roman-script sign says 'Alloy'. Arawy was one of the city's first vegetarian restaurants and it's still going strong, serving good-quality dishes like pumpkin stir-fry.
✉ 152 Th Din So
⏰ 7am-7pm **V**

Baan Phra Arthit Coffee & More (6, B3) $$
Cafe
Homes-away-from-home can be dangerous. Once you've plonked into a big lounge chair and gotten stuck into a game of chess, with great coffee to sustain you, it's hard to pull yourself out. At night the chill-out music gets louder and the lounge lizards become lounge lushes.
✉ 102/1 Th Phra Athit
☎ 02 280 7878
⏰ Mon-Fri 11am-10pm, Sat-Sun 11am-11pm

Banana Leaf Books & Coffee (6, D3) $$
Cafe
Barely a hairbead's throw off Th Khao San is this little outpost of sanity, where you can start the day with a peaceful coffee and end it with a quiet beer and plate of pepper and garlic squid. If you really want to shut out the world, rifle

through the bookshelves for something you fancy (it's also a second-hand bookshop).
✉ 34/1 Th Khao San
☎ 02 629 3343
⏰ 10.30am-11pm ♿

Bangkok Bar (2, B3) $$$
Restaurant-Bar-Gallery
Yes, yet another Bangkok Bar, but this one gets a mention more for its austere surroundings than its Thai food, which is okay but lacks punch for the price. It's in an imposing 19th-century white mansion on Khlong Banglamphu, with garden seats outside and changing modern art exhibitions on the walls inside.
✉ 591 Th Phra Sumen
☎ 02 281 6237
⏰ 6pm-2am

Commé (6, B3) $$
Bar-Restaurant-Gallery
Commé is a master of the arty, student restaurant scene that has taken off in Bangkok. Every night, young fashionable types spill out of its two bars (one fan-cooled, the other one air-conditioned) onto the streets, nibbling endlessly on plates of deep-fried chicken knuckles and *yam plaa dùk fuu* (fried catfish salad) and listening to the live bands.
✉ 1002-6 Th Phra Athit ☎ 02 280 0647
⏰ 4pm-1am

Hemlock (6, C2) $$
Bar-Restaurant
Technically Hemlock is a bar, but to come here and not eat would be an act of unbelievable stupidity. Book a table because *everyone* knows how

amazing the food is. Unravelling and eating the succulent *kài hàw bai toey* (marinated chicken wrapped in pandanus leaf and fried) is almost a religious experience.

✉ **56 Th Phra Athit**
☎ **02 282 7507**
🕐 **Mon-Fri 4pm-midnight, Sat 5pm-midnight** **V**

Street Food

The classic Bangkok eating experience is sitting on a plastic stool by the side of a traffic-choked road and eating a bowl of noodles just cooked by a street-stall vendor. Locals, both rich and poor, will travel any distance to their favourite noodle stall – it's not rare to see Mercedes parked alongside motorbikes.

But it's not just noodles that taste better from street stalls. No matter how good a restaurant's green papaya salad (*sôm-tam*) may be, it's never the same as the one from your *sôm-tam* stall, where you direct just how much chilli and lime juice you want pummelled in the mortar.

The best stalls – for both food and standards of hygiene – are usually crowded with locals. A good rule to follow is: don't eat anything you haven't seen cooked yourself, meaning barbecued meats and pre-cooked curries might be best avoided.

To get the best off the street, teach yourself some basic vocabulary for the best dishes, like:

* *sôm-tam*
* *jòhk*, thick rice soup
* *kuaytiaw nàam*, rice noodle soup with meat and vegetables
* *kuaytiaw phàt thai*, thin rice noodles with tofu, vegetables, egg and peanuts
* *kuaytiaw phàt khîi mao*, wide rice noodles with meat, vegetables, chilli and Thai basil

Food stalls on Soi 4 (Nana Tai)

Himalayan Kitchen
(6, D3) **$$**
Nepalese
Just like Nepal, Himalayan Kitchen has a prime vantage point over the world. Around here, the world is the Khao San parade, which is endlessly amusing to watch while you get stuck into your enormous thali plate, starting with the delicately spiced potato curry.
✉ **1 Th Khao San**
🕐 **8am-1am** ♿ **V**

Isan restaurants
(2, D7) **$**
Isan
When a boxing match is on at nearby Ratchadamnoen Stadium, these simple restaurants are run off their feet serving plates of Isan staples like *kài yàang* (grilled chicken), *sôm-tam* (green papaya salad) and *khào niaw* sticky rice.
✉ **Th Ratchadamnoen Nok** 🕐 **11am-10pm**

Joy Luck Club
(6, B3) **$$**
Bar-Restaurant
Joy Luck Club is a dark, intimate place just off the Th Phra Athit strip. Decorated with dangling red lanterns outside and mismatched memorabilia inside, it only has a few tables, usually taken by couples deep in conversation or engrossed in their food, like *yam plaa mèuk* (spicy squid salad).
✉ **8 Th Phra Sumen**
🕐 **5pm-midnight**

Khrua Nopparat
(6, B3) **$**
Thai
It may have a groovy factor of zilch (not particularly common 'round these parts)

but the food factor rockets off the scale. Local Thai families and workmates usually crowd this joint to eat plates of yummy everyday Thai dishes at little more than street prices.
✉ **136 Th Phra Athit**
☎ **02 281 7578**
🕐 **Mon-Sat 10.30am-9.30pm**

Ricky's Coffee Shop
(6, C2)   **$$**
Cafe
Ricky's is a beautiful cafe, decorated like an old Chinese shopfront and decked out with old fans and cigarette postergirl prints. And it knows its market so well – it serves the best coffee, fruit shakes and Western dishes in

Banglamphu. Pity about the unreliable service and bland Thai food.
✉ **22 Th Phra Athit**
☎ **02 846 3011**
🕐 **8am-midnight** **V**

Roti Mataba (6, B3)   **$**
Malaysian
Don't visit Banglamphu without stopping by Roti Mataba. Even if you're not hungry, you can watch the rhythms of the roti-makers as they slap and flip the Indian-style bread on the hotplate. But it's hard to resist fresh crunchy roti dipped in chicken korma or stuffed with vegetables.
✉ **136 Th Phra Athit**
🕐 **11am-10pm**

Sarah (6, D3)   **$**
Israeli
Sarah is an honest Israeli eatery situated near the end of a laneway running along the side of the petrol station between Th Khao San and Th Rambutri. Usually kebab-to-kebab with homesick travellers tucking into faithful favourites such as felafel, shawarma and schnitzel, it serves iced mint tea with incredible life-restoring properties.
✉ **lane north of Th Khao San** 🕐 **10am-midnight** **V**

Roti Mataba is roti heaven.

Saffron Bakery
(6, C2)   **$**
Cafe
If cream has been sadly missed from your diet in dairy-impaired Bangkok, sneak over to the Saffron Bakery for a big, gooey piece of cake and a cup of coffee. The setting is twee, but in an endearing way, and the pastries are divine.
✉ **Th Phra Athit**
☎ **02 281 4228**
🕐 **10am-8pm** 👟

Ton Pho (6, C2)   **$$**
Thai
On a steamy day, try to catch a breeze at this open-air riverside restaurant, just behind Tha Banglamphu. Ceiling fans rotate relentlessly overhead, as waiters scurry across the wooden floorboards (with big gaps revealing the river beneath) to deliver plate after plate of excellent soups, salads and seafood.
✉ **Th Phra Athit, at Tha Banglamphu**
☎ **02 280 0452**
🕐 **11am-10pm**

Breeze by Ton Pho for soups, salads and seafood.

CHINATOWN & PHAHURAT

The best way to get to these restaurants is to take the river express boat to Tha Ratchawong and Tha Si Phraya (Chinatown) or Th Saphan Phut (Phahurat), or travel by taxi. The bus is far too frustrating.

Hong Kong Dim Sum
(2, K7) $
Chinese
Amid the hustle and bustle of Chinatown's most fascinating laneway is this haven of comfort snacks, of warm, fluffy, barbecued pork buns and buttery, crumbling custard tarts. Grab a few of your dim sum favourites and forge on – all in the name of retail therapy.
✉ **136/5 Trok Itsaranuphap near cnr of Th Charoen Krung**
⏱ 10am-8pm ☗

Hong Kong Noodles
(2, K7) $
Chinese
Unlike its sister restaurant next door, Hong Kong Noodles is a place for pure sustenance, when you simply can't go on any longer. A bowl of noodles (made on the premises) and roast duck in a restorative broth should do the trick.
✉ **136/4 Trok Itsaranuphap**
⏱ 10am-8pm ☗

Kou Mueng Deam
(2, K4) $
Thai
After a crazy morning at the nearby Pak Khlong and Phahurat markets, retreat to this cool little haven. Run by young Thai guys, it's in a restored Chinatown-style shop, complete with rickety ceiling fans, marble floors and stained-glass windows. The food is feisty and authentic.
✉ **Th Atsadang**

Old Siam Plaza Food Centre

☎ **02 222 9038**
⏱ **Mon-Thur 10.30am-10.30pm, Fri-Sat 10.30am-midnight**

Krisa Coffee Shop
(2, G3) $
Thai
Krisa Coffee Shop is a nifty pitstop during a hot and hard-going trek around the temples and palaces of Ratanakosin – it's air-conditioned and serves up cheap and cheerful one-plate meals, like *kuay tiaw phàt kîi mao* (wide rice noodles with holy basil and chilli), to see you through the expedition.
✉ **Th Na Phra Lan**
⏱ 10am-8pm ☗

Old Siam Plaza Food Centre (2, J5) $
Food hall
The architects behind the Old Siam Plaza building were trying to revive the Ratanakosin style of architecture, where traditional Thai concepts were mixed with European. Fortunately, there's very little European influence in this handy food hall, filled with stalls selling Chinese and Thai favourites.
✉ **cnr Th Phahurat & Th Triphet**
⏱ 10am-5pm ☗

Pet Tun Jao Tha
(2, N9) $
Chinese
As the name 'Harbour Department Stewed Duck' suggests, big birds are the order of the day here. You don't have to just eat the special – steamed duck and goose with rice

Strictly Vegetarian
It's tough to be truly vegetarian at Thai restaurants. You can ask for 'no meat or seafood' but then your dish arrives with fish sauce. But you won't need to worry at strictly vegetarian places like Arawy (p. 75) and Khun Churn (p. 86) or Indian restaurants like Standard Sweets (p. 79) and Chennai Kitchen (p. 85). Don't miss Chinatown during its annual Vegetarian Festival.

noodles – but you'd be silly not to. This restaurant is at the far eastern edge of Chinatown, down near River City.

✉ **392/1 Chak Phet Rd**
🕐 **11am-8pm** ♿ **V**

Royal India (2, K5) $$
North Indian
You are unsure as you wander down the dark laneway and open an unmarked door. Inside tables of men are deep in discussion while a voluptuously moustachioed Indian man flogs golf clubs on cable TV. You soon discover the food is absolutely incredible and the dhal indescribably delicious. Mission accomplished.

✉ **392/1 Th Chakraphet**
☎ **02 221 656**
🕐 **10am-10pm V**

Shangarila
(2, K7) $$$
Cantonese
Got a Peking duck craving? Haven't had a grand, slap-up Cantonese meal for a while? Don't look past Shangarila, one of Chinatown's most respected restaurants. Chinese families from around the city come to spin the lazy Susan during its famed dim sum lunches.

✉ **206 Th Yaowarat**
☎ **02 235 7493**
🕐 **11am-10pm** ♿ **V**

Standard Sweets
(2, K5) $
South Indian
If you need some sustenance during a serious Phahurat market expedition, stop by this barebones Punjabi place for a

Shangarila – dim sum mecca

paneer dosa. The guys cook them on a hotplate in the alley, crammed with spice, grocery and sari shops, which runs beside the ATM department store.

✉ **95/57-67 Th Chakraphet, Phahurat**
🕐 **10am-10pm** ♿ **V**

White Orchid Restaurant (2, K8) $$
Chinese
Even if you're used to the point-and-order method, it can be unsettling selecting your dim sum from 20 baskets filled with plastic imitation food of dubious artistic quality. But persevere because you'll be soon be congratulating yourself on your excellent judgement, like the succulent prawn dumplings and minced crab rolls.

✉ **2nd fl, White Orchid Hotel, 409-21 Th Yaowarat, Chinatown**
☎ **02 226 0026**
🕐 **10.30am-11pm** ♿

Dim Sum
Bangkok's big Chinese population means that there are some excellent dim sum options. Get your chopsticks around the dumplings at: China House (p. 87), Mei Jiang (p. 88), Shagarila (p. 79) and White Orchid (p. 79).

So much to eat, so little time, Chinatown

SUKHUMVIT

The Skytrain has made eating out in Sukhumvit much easier. You can also catch a bus down Th Sukhumvit to Soi 21 (air-con No 1, 8, 11, 13) or farther down to the bigger-numbered sois (air-con No 1, 2, 8, 11, 13, 38).

Akbar (3, C13)   **$$**
Bangladeshi-Indian-Iranian-Pakistani
Connoisseurs of Indian restaurant design will know they've found a winner in Akbar, where the design brief was 'too much is never enough' and the owner, brandishing Elvisesque sideburns, strolls around as if he's on a Florida golf course. For more sensory overload, try the tangy cheese and potato kofta in spinach.
✉ 1/4 Soi 3, Th Sukhumvit ☎ 02 253 3479 ⏰ 10.30am-midnight [V]

The Atlanta Coffee Shop (3, E13)   **$$**
Thai
We could rave on until the cows come home. The Atlanta is not only the grooviest coffee shop in town, with a decor straight out of the 1950s, but it also takes its vegetarian Thai food seriously (you will never read a more intense menu, nor taste a

better fried morning glory). The breakfasts are great, too.
✉ 78 Soi 2, Th Sukhumvit ☎ 02 252 6069 ⏰ 6am-11pm ♿ [V]

Al Nakhil (3, D12)   **$$**
Lebanese
Just outside the supermarket at the Ploenchit Centre, this basic Lebanese eatery is a popular place to pick up a quick felafel kebab or snack on some Lebanese bread and creamy hummus. Small, cheap and simple.
✉ Ploenchit Centre, cnr Soi 2 & Th Sukhumvit
⏰ 10am-8pm [V]

basil (3, E15)   **$$$$**
Thai
Set aside a few hours for the basil experience. Nothing is done by halves – even the rice comes in three varieties – and the food is deservedly among the city's best. Durian virgins: take the plunge with the durian cheesecake. You'll never forget the first time.
✉ Sheraton Grande Sukhumvit, 250 Th Sukhumvit, btw Sois 12 & 14 ☎ 02 653 0333 ⏰ 11.30am-2pm & 6-10pm

Bei Otto (4, C2)   **$$$**
German
Proudly German right down to its sausage placemats, Bei Otto is where misty-eyed expats come for roasted pigs knuckle (actually, everyone comes for that), proper bread and a frothy stein of wheatbeer. Otto's slowly expanding empire now encompasses a bar and restaurant (serving the same food) and a delicatessen.
✉ 1 Soi 20, Th Sukhumvit
☎ 02 262 0892
⏰ 9am-1am ♿

Table at basil awaits the deflowering of a durian virgin.

Crickets to Go

Unlike Westerners, who like don't like the combination of food and insects, the Thais don't mind the odd snack of deep-fried crickets. If you fancy a bag of crickets, some red ants or water beetles (they look like cockroaches), stop by the stall on Soi 4, Th Sukhumvit.

Crepes & Co
(3, E14) $$$
French-Moroccan
It sounds like it should be a suburban pancake franchise (can we buy the formula?) but Crepes & Co is an original, much-loved by brunch buffs. You could do worse than lingering in the leafy courtyard all day and then staying for dinner (and the rich fish tagine is worth waiting for).
✉ 18/1 Soi 12, Th Sukhumvit ☎ 02 653 3990 ⏱ 9am-midnight V

Greyhound Cafe
(4, C3) $$
Cafe
Don't be fooled by the flimsy fashionista types picking at their pasta and the minimalism du jour of the design. The Greyhound Cafe is undoubtedly a very cool place to be seen but the food (Thai and fusion cafe favourites) is fantastic. Also at Central Chitlom, Zen.
✉ 2nd fl, The Emporium, btw Sois 22 & 24, Th Sukhumvit ☎ 02 664 8663 ⏱ 11am-10pm

Foodland (3, C13) $
Thai
The noodle and stir-fry bar at Foodland supermarket has a fond place in the heart of many a hardcore clubber or barfly – not because the food is out of this world, but because it's open when the munchies hit.
✉ btw Sois 3/1 & 5, Th Sukhumvit ☎ 02 530 0220 ⏱ 24 hrs V

Kuppa (3, G15) $$$$
Cafe
Kuppa is *the* hot spot for young, rich Thais (especially at weekend brunchtimes), who leave their drivers sleeping in the BMW while they tuck into braised lambshanks with lentils. Converted from an industrial space, Kuppa is light and airy, with a menu dominated by reliable Italian and fusion dishes.
✉ 39 Soi 16, Th Sukhumvit ☎ 02 2258 1782 ⏱ Tues-Sun 10.30am-10.30pm ♿

Le Dalat Indochine
(4, B2) $$$
Vietnamese
The exquisite Vietnamese food almost gets sidelined by the divine surroundings at Le Dalat Indochine, where you eat in a beautifully converted old house, filled with potted palms and artworks. Try the house special, *naem meuang*, grilled meatballs mixed with spices and fruit on ricepaper rolls, then wrapped in lettuce.
✉ 47/1 Soi 23, Th Sukhumvit ☎ 02 258 4192 ⏱ 11am-2.30pm & 5-10pm ♿

Mrs Balbir's
(3, D14) $$$
North Indian
Mrs Balbir is a one-woman empire and entertainment machine, spanning a TV show, cooking school (see p. 46) and this famous Sukhumvit eatery. Her larger-than-life personality is the reason many people

come here to eat – the North Indian food is good but not outstanding.
✉ **155/18 Soi 11/1, Th Sukhumvit** ☎ **02 651 0498** ⏲ **Tues-Sun noon-10.30pm** ♿ **V**

Nasir al-Masri Restaurant & Shishah (3, C13) $$
Egyptian
If there was ever a place to wear your sunglasses at night, Nasir al-Masri is it. Reflections off walls of mirrors, glass tabletops and silver furnishings created a virtual laser show as we munched on fluffy Egyptian bread and spicy lamb chops. Light-sensitive types: try the cushion-lined hookah room upstairs.
✉ **4/6 Sukhumvit Soi 3/1, Pathumwan** ☎ **02 253 5582** ⏲ **7am-4am** ♿

Salon de L'Oriental (4, D4) $$
Cafe
People-watching is at a premium at the fountain-side seats, usually occupied by ladies who lunch and princesses who shop. If you don't make it to the Oriental Hotel's high tea, this is a backup option – the scones and cucumber sarnies arrive, like they

Breakfast Is Served
If your tastebuds can't handle traditional Thai or Chinese breakfasts, try these spots: Crepes & Co (p. 81; for a leafy, languid breakfast), the Colonnade (p. 85; for indulgence), Atlanta Coffee Shop (p. 80; for jazz and the papers), Kuppa (p. 81; for trendy brunch) and Coffee Society (p. 85; for a quick coffee and pastry).

Kick-start your day at Atlanta Coffee Shop.

should, on a silver-tiered server.
✉ **ground fl, The Emporium, btw Sois 22 & 24, Th Sukhumvit** ☎ **02 664 8186** ⏲ **Mon-Fri 10.30am-10pm, Sat & Sun 10am-10pm**

The Emporium Food Court (4, D4) $
Thai & Chinese
This is probably the classiest food hall you'll ever eat in (it even comes with sweep-ing views of Benchasiri Park), though it's by far the cheapest eating option in this centre, besides the fast-food joints. The food is classic eat-and-run fodder – it's good but unremarkable.
✉ **5th fl, The Emporium, btw Sois 22 & 24, Th Sumhumvit** ☎ **02 664 8000** ⏲ **11am-10pm** ♿

Vientiane Kitchen (4, E5) $$
Isan
Night after night, this open-air barn is alive with Lao music, dancing and the chatter of families sitting at low tables. But the vibe comes second to the authentic Isan specialities, like frog *laap* (minced frog salad), *gài yàng* (grilled marinated chicken) and the ubiquitous sticky rice.
✉ **8 Soi 36, Th Sukhumvit** ☎ **02 258 6171** ⏲ **11am-mid-night** ♿

SIAM SQUARE

This category also includes restaurants in the areas around Th Ploenchit, Th Ratchadamri and Th Withayu. Use the Skytrain to get around if you can or else catch buses along Th Withayu (No 62, 76) or Th Ratchadamri (air-con No 4, 5, 15).

Baan Khanitha & Gallery (3, E12) $$$
Thai
Baan Khanitha is one of Bangkok's classic restaurants, though this branch is only a few years old. Why? It's got the formula down pat – outstanding food, high-class setting, challenging art gallery and impeccable service. Don't risk not making a booking. Also at Soi 23, Th Sukhumvit.
✉ **49 Soi Ruam Rudi 2, Th Ploenchit** ☎ **02 253 4638-9** ⊙ **10.30am-2pm & 6-11pm** ♿

Fabb Fashion Café (3, C10) $$$$
Italian
This place just can't get over how cool it is. Waiters wield enormous pepper grinders, beautiful young things gossip over a plate of lobster salad and live jazz tinkles away in the background. Sure, the food and jazz is good but the coffee could be much better for the price and attitude.
✉ **Mercury Tower, 540 Th Ploenchit** ☎ **02 658 6200** ⊙ **10am-1pm (jazz from 8pm)**

Grappino Italian Restaurant (3, A9) $$$$
Italian
Grappino has got soul. Like an Italian, it takes its wining and dining experience seriously, so it makes the pasta and bread from

> ## Food Without the Fumes
> Eating freshly cooked meals at the food halls in Bangkok's shopping arcades, like the Emporium (p. 59) and MBK (p. 59), is a more lung-friendly option to eating on the street. You buy food with coupons, paid for at special booths. You can refund any unspent coupons – but only on the day of purchase.

scratch, has a cellar to die for and always has a fun, vivacious vibe. It even prides itself on its extensive grappa collection – a sure sign that the heart leads the head here.
✉ **Amari Watergate Hotel, 847 Th Phetburi, Pratunam** ☎ **02 653 9000** ⊙ **noon-2.30pm & 6-11pm**

MBK Food Hall (3, C6) $
Chinese-Thai
It's like having all your favourite street food-vendors in one place – you don't need to visit the noodle woman in one street, the fruit-juice man in another and then find a

mango and sticky rice stall. From 3pm, the view from the open-air beer garden makes cheap beer taste even better.
✉ **6th floor, MBK shopping centre, cnr Th Phra Ram I & Th Phayathai** ⊙ **10am-midnight** ♿ **V**

Sara-Jane's (3, E11) $$
Isan-Italian
Don't be fooled by the soulless office-building surroundings and Italian food on the menu: Sara-Jane's knows its Isan food. That's why expats and Thais keep coming back for the juicy, flavoursome *laap* and *yam sôm oh* (pomelo

Coffee's not ab-fab at Fabb Fashion Café.

and wicker baskets. But most importantly the spice theme is translated into delectable food.

✉ **Regent Bangkok, 155 Ratchadamri Rd** ☎ **02 251 6127** ⏰ **11.30am-2.30pm & 6-11pm**

Whole Earth

(3, D10) $$
Indian-Thai

Reclining on cushions upstairs, you feel like you're in your New Agey auntie's lounge room, decorated with souvenirs from her 'getting spiritual' tour of Asia in the 1970s. And, when you think about it, the vegetarian food's a bit like that too – homy, familiar and nutritious, but fairly unexciting. Except for the divine fruit lassis.

✉ **93/3 Soi Lang Suan** ☎ **252 5574** ⏰ **11.30am-2pm & 5.30-11pm** ⚥ **V**

salad) – though you could order any Isan dish and quite easily go into raptures of delight.

✉ **ground fl, Sindhorn Tower 1, 130-2 Th Withayu** ☎ **02 650 9992-3** ⏰ **11am-9pm**

Sorn's (3, B6) $$

Thai-International

A pair of mad Siamese cats scampering through the garden is about as action-packed as it gets at this lazy and somewhat shambolic garden cafe. Sorn's is a popular breakfast spot

for travellers staying at the handful of guesthouses on this street.

✉ **36/8 Soi Kasem San 1, Th Phra Ram I, Siam Sq** ☎ **02 215 5163** ⏰ **7am-1pm & 5-10pm**

Spice Market

(3, D9) $$$$
Thai

Spice Market is a theme restaurant, but not the sort you're thinking – this is the Regent Hotel, after all. It's based on the old-style Thai spice markets, with wooden shelves, sacks of spices

SILOM

The Skytrain is also your best bet for getting around the Silom district, which also includes areas around Th Surawong (catch bus No 1, 16, 35, 36, 75, 93) and Th Sathon Tai (catch bus No 17, 22, 62, 67, 106, 116, 149).

Alliance Française

(3, J9) $
Cafe

It's fun to watch a cliche in action. The clientele at this simple, popular French cafe live up to every Gallic stereotype – they take their food seriously, smoke furiously, gesticulate wildly and argue about politics. The food – buttery pastries, good coffee and crunchy baguettes – is predictably French, too.

✉ **29 Th Sathon Tai, Silom** ☎ **02 670 4200** ⏰ **11am-2pm** ⚥

Anna's Cafe

(3, G8) $$$
Thai-International

The owners of the four Anna's Cafes were so inspired by Anna Leon Owens (Rama IV's governess of *The King & I* fame) that they named their upmarket restaurant chain after her. Avowed sweet tooths will swear this branch, the first, has the city's best desserts (everyone raves about the banoffee pie).

✉ **118 Soi Sala Daeng, Th Silom** ☎ **02 632**

0619-20 ⏰ **11am-11pm**

Bussaracum

(3, J4) $$$
Thai

Royal Thai cuisine at its skilful best. Bussaracum (pronounced 'boot-sa-ra-kam') creates its intricate dishes from scratch and then presents them like works of art, so much so it (almost) breaks your heart digging a fork and spoon into your delicate purple dumpling flowers, and dramatically carved squash gourd overflowing with seafood.

✉ **Sethiwan Tower, 139 Soi Pan, Th Silom** ☎ **02-266 6312** ⏰ **11am-2pm & 5-11pm**

Celadon (3, H9) $$$$
Thai

Celadon is an effortless dining experience, two elegant pavilions perched atop serene lotus ponds. Stylishly executed Thai favourites are served on delicate celadon crockery, as well as more inventive dishes like the starter plate.

✉ **Sukhothai, 13/3 Th Sathorn Thai** ☎ **02 287 0222** ⏰ **11.30am-2.30pm & 6.30-10.30pm**

Chennai Kitchen (3, J4) $
South Indian

Just down the road from the rowdy Sri Mariamman temple, Chennai Kitchen is a Southern Indian outpost (vegetarians rejoice!) in a land where tandoori, rather than dosa, rules the roost.

✉ **48/6 Soi Pan, Th Silom** ☎ **02 238 4141** ⏰ **10am-3pm & 6-9.30pm** **V**

Coffee Society (3, G8) $$
Cafe

If you like aesthetics with your caffeine hit, look no further than Coffee Society, a dark, modern-Asian-style cafe in neon Silom. And with late closing hours, it's ideal for a juicy post-party post-mortem or refuelling stop.

✉ **18 Th Silom** ☎ **02 235 9784** ⏰ **Mon-Sat 8.30-4am, Sun 8.30am-11pm**

Ahem, elegant Celadon

Colonnade (3, H9) $$$$
International

Colonnade should be awarded a medal for its untiring, relentless dedication to decadence. Every day between 2.30pm and 6pm, it trots out its chocolate buffet (verging on chocolate porn). Then on Sunday buffets have to be lined with caviar, imported cheeses, foie gras for the jazz brunch from noon.

✉ **13/3 Th Sathon Tai, Silom** ☎ **02 287 0222** ⏰ **6am-midnight** ♿

Eat Me (3, H7) $$$
International

Eat Me is one of Bangkok's most innovative and interesting restaurants. It throws together smart fusion dishes (like soft shell crab and linguini), cutting edge artworks and the smooth modern design and comes up trumps night after night. Book for a balcony table on live jazz nights (Thursday and Saturday).

✉ **1/6 Soi Piphat 2 (off Th Convent), Silom** ☎ **02 238 0931** ⏰ **3pm-1am**

Jim Thompson Cafe & Farmers Market (3, H9) $$
Thai

The farmers market concept – where plants and vegetables from the restaurant garden were for

---

Late-Night Eats

You'll never go hungry in Bangkok at any hour of the day or night. You should always be able to find a noodle stall. For other late (or early) snacks, try: Foodland Supermarket's noodle bar (p. 81; open 24hrs), Coffee Society (p. 85; usually open until 4am) or any bar (open until 2am) which serves great food, like Commé (p. 75) and Tapas (p. 93).

Coffee Society – for a civilised caffeine fix

Kozi Sushi – chopsticks at the ready, set, go…

sale – was interesting but has died off, a rare false move for the Jim Thompson brand. So this pleasant cafe has stuck steadfastly to what it knows best: reliable Thai food in civilised surroundings.

✉ **120/1 Soi 1, Th Sala Daeng** ☎ **02 266 9167** ⏱ **9am-9pm**

Khun Churn (3, J5) $
Thai
Vegetarians and vegans, you can relax and enjoy yourselves. You won't have to worry about getting fish sauce in your salad or egg tossed in your noodles at Khun Churn. Grab a garden table and peruse the vast menu, including

Great Places to Do Business
To close a really important business deal, go for one of the five-star hotel restaurants like Angelini (p. 87), Grappino (p. 83) or Le Normandie (p. 88). But if you're after a less flashy and more low-key place to wine and dine clients, you could try Anna's Cafe (p. 84) or Kuppa (p. 81).

'pseudo' Chinese favourites, like mock duck and fake sharkfin soup.

✉ **64 Soi 10, Th Sathon Tai** ☎ **02 237 0800** ⏱ **9.30am-2.30pm & 4.30-8.30pm** **V**

Kozi Sushi (3, G7) $$
Japanese
If you need some purity in your diet, become a trainspotter along the sushi train tracks of this restaurant. But be prepared for some duelling chopsticks during the hugely popular 220B all-you-can-eat lunch at this venue just off the Japanese entertainment strip of Soi Thaniya.

✉ **ground fl, Thaniya Plaza, Soi Thaniya, Th Silom** ☎ **02 231 2918** ⏱ **11.30am-2pm & 5.30-11pm**

Le Cafe Siam (3, J12) $$$
French-Thai
Aglow with glass lanterns and fairy lights and humming with live jazz, Le Cafe Siam is magical at night (but to avoid a magical mystery tour getting here, take a taxi). Lots of people rave about this restaurant, but the prawn and mushroom salad lacked the flavour and flair you'd

expect for the price.

✉ **4 Soi Sri Akson, off Soi Sri Bamphen** ☎ **02 671 0030-1** ⏱ **11am-2pm & 6pm-2am** ♿

Mango Tree (3, G6) $$
Thai
A little corner of peace in the pumping, grinding pace of Silom. The formula sounds familiar – well-executed traditional fare, the quiet plonkings of Thai musicians and historical decor – but it's pulled off with a rare flair. Don't miss the *plaa samlii dáet diaw* (cottonfish with mango salad).

✉ **37 Soi Than Tawan, Th Surawong** ☎ **02 236 2820** ⏱ **11.30am-10pm** ♿

Somboon Seafood (3, G7) $$$
Chinese Seafood
The surroundings are nothing to write home about, but you won't want to go home once you have a big bowl of the famous crab curry. If you don't fancy getting messy with crab curry, Somboon does a mean whole fried fish.

✉ **169/7-11 Th Surawong** ☎ **02 234 4499** ⏱ **4-11.30pm** ♿

Sphinx (3, G7) $$
Thai
Sphinx may be Bangkok's most popular gay restaurant, but foodies are keeping an eye on this turf as well. The food is so consistently good (especially the nutty, tangy wingbean salad) that there could be an outbreak of turf wars any day now.

✉ **100 Soi 4, Th Silom** ☎ **02 234 7249** ⏱ **6pm-2am**

RIVERSIDE

By Riverside, we mean the area along Mae Nam Chao Phraya in the south-west of the old city, both on the Bangkok and Thonburi banks. All the restaurants can be reached from the Saphan Taksin Skytrain station or Tha Sathorn express boat jetty.

Angelini (3, J2) **$$$$**
Italian
Angelini manages to be simultaneously grand and relaxed. It could easily be too posh for words, what with such high prices (for excellent Italian dishes, mind you) and extravagant decor, but somehow the riverside location just brings it down to earth nicely.
✉ **ground fl, Shangri-La Wing, Shangri-La Hotel, 89 Soi Wat Suan Plu, Bangrak**
☎ **02 236 7777**
◷ **11am-midnight**

Ban Chiang (3, J4) **$$**
Thai
Hot chips will never again satisfy your cravings for something fried and crunchy once you've eaten the *yam plaa dúk fuu* (salad with fried grated catfish) at Ban Chiang. The other isan specialities served in this atmospheric wooden Thai house are just

Hotel Restaurants? No Worries!
You can't afford to have snobberies about hotel restaurant food in Bangkok. The city's five-star hotel restaurants break the mould – in fact, it's hard to find one of Australia's or Europe's top chefs who hasn't done a stint in a Bangkok hotel.

Buffet lunch at Sheraton Grande

as lip-smacking good.
✉ **14 Soi Si Wiang, Th Surasak** ☎ **02 236 7045** ◷ **11am-2pm & 5-10.30pm** ♿

China House (2, P9) **$$$$**
Cantonese
The oh-so-formal surrounds and the waitresses – in

cheongsams slashed to the thigh – and their aloof manner may disarm you, but don't let that distract you from the best quality, best value dim sum in town. The scallop dumpling in heavenly broth is truly unforgettable.
✉ **Soi Oriental, Th Charoen Krung**
☎ **02 659 9000**
◷ **11.30am-2.30pm & 6.30-10.30pm**

Harmonique (2, O9) **$$**
Chinese-Thai
You can get jaded after you've eaten in umpteen gorgeous Thai houses. Another bloody beautiful wooden building with nice bloody Buddhas and traditional artefacts, you think. Somehow Harmonique manages to transcend the formula with

its own haphazard style. Maybe it's the crazy owner who treats waiting as his daily exercise.

✉ **22 Soi 34, Th Charoen Krung** ☎ **02 630 6763** ⏰ **Mon-Sat 11am-10pm**

Himali Cha-Cha
(2, P10) $$

North Indian

No Latin dancing here, just solid North Indian food at solid prices. Actually, the name comes from the founder – yes, Cha-Cha – who worked as a chef for India's last viceroy but has handed over the pots and pans to his son.

✉ **1229/11 Th Charoen Krung** ☎ **02 235 1569** ⏰ **11am-3.30pm & 6-10.30pm** **V**

Indian Hut
(2, P10) $$$

North Indian

Paneer, paneer, paneer. We can't stress it enough – don't dare leave Indian Hut without trying its home-made cottage cheese, preferably in the deceptively simple tomato and onion curry. Despite the fast-food overtones in the name, this place is classy and popular with businesspeople.

✉ **311/2-5 Th Surawong** ☎ **02 237 8812** ⏰ **11am-3pm & 6.30-10.30pm**

Le Normandie
(2, P9) $$$$

French

Give yourself time to prepare for Le Normandie, one of Bangkok's finest. Make sure the jacket and tie are drycleaned and the booking is confirmed. Discipline your stomach and get your mind ready for some big decisions – the degustation or roast lobster with java beans, home-made egg noodles and bisque sauce?

✉ **Oriental Hotel, Soi Oriental, Th Charoen Krung** ☎ **02 236 0400** ⏰ **Mon-Sat noon-2.30pm & 7-10.30pm**

Mei Jiang **(3, J1)** $$$$

Cantonese

Quite intentionally, the Peninsula has sited Mei Jiang on its ground floor, a good 20 storeys away from sweeping city vistas. The aim is to make you focus on internal matters, namely the Art Deco-influenced interior design and the inside of your stomach, which will be eagerly anticipating the Peking duck.

✉ **Peninsula Hotel, 333 Th Charoen Nakhon, Thonburi** ☎ **02 861 2888** ⛴ **hotel shuttle boat from Tha Sathorn** ⏰ **Mon-Sat 11.30am-2.30pm & 6-10pm, Sun 11am-2.30pm & 6-10pm**

Tongue Thai
(2, P9) $$

Thai

Maybe the name is supposed to remind us of the chef's honourable intentions to not sacrifice Thai flavours to Western palates. Anyway, your tongue will be feeling most Thai as it wraps itself around flavoursome morsels of spicy eggplant salad.

✉ **18-20 Soi 38, Th Charoen Krung** ☎ **02 630 9918-9** ⏰ **11am-11pm** **V**

High Tea

High tea is such an institution in Bangkok, you'd have thought Thailand was colonised. Tea in the Oriental Hotel's Author's Lounge (p. 40) is all potted plants, cane furniture and tiered silver servers. The Regent Bangkok (p. 103) offers grand surroundings and a string quartet, while the Colonnade (p. 85) has an indecently divine chocolate buffet. High tea goes from around 2.30-6pm.

Don't be a Coward, try Oriental Hotel's Author's Lounge.

GREAT VIEWS

Other restaurants where you won't be able to keep your eyes from wandering include the riverside Ton Pho, Kaloang Home Kitchen and Angelini, The Emporium Food Court with views over Benjasiri Park and Celadon, where you gaze out onto lotus ponds.

Rang Mahal
(4, C2)   **$$$**
South Indian
Baby, it's cold inside. There are grand white columns, luxurious furnishings and air-conditioning of an Arctic-style chill factor. But get stuck into the curries, considered Bangkok's best, and you'll be warm again. Go for the Sunday brunch or at night when the city lights look magical from up here.
✉ **19 Soi 18, Th Sukhumvit** ☎ **02 261 7100** 🚇 **Asok** 🚌 **air-con 1, 2, 8, 11, 13, 38** ⏰ **Mon-Sat 11.30am-2.30pm & 6.30-10pm, Sun 11am-3pm** 🅥

Tiara (3, G8)   **$$$$**
International
Tiara really is the crown of the Dusit Thani hotel – it's on the very top floor. Fortunately it's in the greenest part of the Bangkok concrete jungle, so you can gaze out onto Lumphini Park.
✉ **Dusit Thani, 946 Th Phra Ram IV** ☎ **02 236 9999** 🚇 **Sala Daeng** ⏰ **11am-2.30pm & 6-10pm** 🍴 **kids' brunch Sun**

WORTH A TRIP

Kaloang Home Kitchen (2, A5)   **$$**
Seafood
Rough and rustic, Kaloang Home Kitchen serves excellent seafood dishes – the deep-fried snakehead fish is yet to be surpassed, say some – in a quiet position by the river and a royal boat flotilla. Follow Th Sri Ayuthaya right to its western end.
✉ **2 Th Sri Ayuthaya, Dusit** ☎ **02 281 9228** 🚌 **air-con 5** ⚓ **Tha Thewes** ⏰ **11am-11pm**

Pickle Factory
(1, G3)   **$$**
International
Take a taxi to the Pickle Factory, otherwise the long walk that awaits down a dark and pavementless street will sorely taint your appreciation of the retro poolside setting. This establishment did indeed enter this world as a pickle factory of sorts, however, it is now renowned for its studenty vibe as well as its East-meets-West pizzas (of which the Chiang Mai sausage variety comes most highly recommended).
✉ **55 Soi 21, Th Ratchawithi, Victory Monument** ☎ **02 246 3036** 🚇 **Victory Monument** ⏰ **5.30-11.30pm**

Taurus Brewhouse
(1, B5)   **$$**
German-International
If you're hanging around Bangkok International Airport, you might as well linger in this German-style brewery restaurant. It's usually busy with execs sipping a frothy house Pilsener while tapping away on their laptop or safari-suited waiters serving up plates of sausages to jetsetters.
✉ **4th fl, terminal 2, Bangkok International Airport** ☎ **02 535 6090** 🚇 **suburban train to Don Muang** 🚌 **airport express A-1, A-2, A-3, A-4** ⏰ **9-3am**

entertainment

Bangkok was truly the city that never slept – until the government's crackdown that, for the first time, strictly enforced 2am closing times. Sex shows (are supposed to) have been cleaned up, regular drugs searches are made of venues and patrons are checked for identification to prove they're over 20. This new social conservatism has taken a swipe at the 'anything goes' attitude, encompassing everything from midget-on-motorbike sex shows to drinking beer while sitting on a plastic milkcrate on a flooded soi at 4am, that made Bangkok one of the world's wildest nightlife scenes. But it hasn't diluted the locals' enthusiastic pursuit of *sanuk*, or fun – these days, they just head out earlier than midnight.

Soi Thaniya, Patpong, is all a go-go.

The Silom area is best known for the Patpong go-go bars (3, G7) but savvy barflies head to Soi 4 (3, G7), a big street party crammed with lady-boys, gays and straights and overflowing with bars, or Soi 2 (3, G8), a tiny, hardcore gay strip. Closeby, Soi Thaniya (3, G7) is the domain of drunk Japanese businessmen all-consumed with young girls dressed like prom queens and nurses who chant for their attention. In Banglamphu, head for vibrant Th Phra Athit (2, D3), lined with groovy little bars-cum-restaurants that are crowded with Thai students. One thing you'll notice about Bangkok entertainment venues is that food is never very far away. Thais love their food and you won't see them hanging around any bar where the food is bad. They also love trends, jumping from new cool venue to new cool venue which means that a place can be rocking one week and deserted the next.

Musician, Erawan Shrine

Even if you value your beauty sleep and your liver, there's plenty to keep you amused once the sun goes down. Become seduced by the enchanting rhythms and artistry of a traditional dance or theatre show. Let theatrics of a *muay thai* boxing match, both inside and outside the ring, mesmerise you. Or kick back in a big lounge chair and snap your fingers to world-class jazz in an all-too-cosy bar.

SPECIAL EVENTS

There's always something going on in Bangkok – check the TAT website (**e** www.tat.or.th) for dates. These festivities are always fascinating and fun:

February *Magha Puja* – a Buddhist festival which ends with a candlelit walk around the main chapels at the city's temples.

February-March *Chinese New Year* – Thai-Chinese all over Bangkok celebrate their lunar new year, with a week of house-cleaning, lion dances and fire-works. Head to Chinatown for the best festivities.

March *Kite-Flying Season* – the skies over Sanam Luang and Lumphini Park are filled with colourful, animal-shaped kites.

April *Songkhran Festival* – water stars in this festival celebrating the lunar new year. Everyone gets wet and wild as pictures at left and below demonstrate.

May *Royal Ploughing Ceremony* – the king takes part in this ancient Brahman ritual at Sanam Luang which kicks off the official rice-planting season.

Visakha Puja – falls on the day that is considered the Buddha's birth, enlightenment and passing away. The action centres around the temples, with plenty of chanting and candlelit processions.

July *Khao Phansâa* – the beginning of Buddhist Lent, this holiday starts the season when young men enter the monkhood for the rainy season and for all monks to base themselves in a monastery for a while. You might see Buddhist ordinations.

September *Thailand International Swan-Boat Races* – held on the river, near the Rama IX Bridge.

October-November *Thawt Kathin* – during this month-long period at the end of the Buddhist phansâa, new monastic robes and requisites are offered to the Sangha.

November *Loi Kràthong* – a beautiful festival where on the night of the full moon, small lotus-shaped baskets or boats made of banana leaf containing a lit candle are floating on the river.

December *King's Birthay* – locals celebrate their monarch's birthday with fervour and lots of twinkling lights.

BARS & PUBS

Bangkok has a diverse bar scene, fed by the student culture in Banglamphu and party-hardy attitude in Silom. Many great Banglamphu bars – like Commé, Baan Phra Arthit Coffee & More, Joy Luck Club and Ricky's Coffee Shop – are also great restaurants, so we've listed them in Places to Eat.

About Studio/About Cafe (2, L9)

Once you've sunk into an enormously fat lounge chair and have a drink in your hand, you can forgive About for being so damned out of the way. Then you remember a visit is always rewarding, whether you're checking out the art upstairs, listening to a poetry reading or just keeping an eye on that retro chair you fancy.
✉ 402-8 Th Maitrichit, Hualamphong
☎ 02 623 1742-3
🚉 suburban train to Hualamphong 🚌 53
🕐 Mon-Sat noon-midnight

Bangkok Bar (6, C3)

There's always a fun vibe at this good-time bar in the heart of Banglamphu. You can play pool, get stuck into great food or just dance like an idiot – and no-one will look at you twice.
✉ 149 Soi Rambutri,

Th Chakraphong, Banglamphu ☎ 02 629 4443 🚌 air-con 6, 17 ⚓ Tha Banglamphu 🕐 7pm-2am

The Barbican (3, G7)

What's a flash pub like you doing in a place like this? The sleek Barbican is surrounded on all sides by Thaniya 'entertainment venues', meaning you can keep a quiet eye on the weird mating rituals outside while you have a quiet beer (or rowdy, if the after-work crowd has arrived).
✉ 9/4-5 Soi Thaniya, Th Silom, Silom ☎ 02 234 3590 🚉 Sala Daeng 🚌 air-con 2, 4, 5, 15 🕐 11.30-2am

Cafe Democ (2, F5)

Serious fans of electronica love this bar and its beats. If you don't want to dance, lounge around upstairs or just linger around the downstairs bar, lined with overhead retro lights. Like most Banglamphu bars, Cafe Democ (named for nearby Democracy Monument) is a big student hang-out.
✉ 78 Th Ratchadamnoen, Banglamphu ☎ 02 622 2571 🚌 air-con 3, 6, 9, 11, 12, 15, 17, 39, 44, 68, 153 🕐 Tues-Sun 4pm-2am

Dog Days (6, B3)

A dog-gone good little bar with an unashamedly canine theme (one wall features a gallery of doggy pictures). If that doesn't grab your interest, maybe the lure of cheap drinks or the design qualities of the stripey wallpaper, just like that snazzy tie your dad wore in the 70s, will.
✉ 100/2-6 Th Phra Athit, Banglamphu

Emerging Ekamai

Young Thais are a fickle bunch, leaving last month's hot spot stone-cold empty to move onto the next. So that's why we recommend barflys keep an eye in the listings press on happenings on Soi Ekamai (Soi 63) off Th Sukhumvit. For a while no one could get enough of its cool bars – especially places like Bangkok Bar (61 Soi 2, off Soi Ekamai), Skunk (Soi 2, off Soi Ekamai) and Bar Baska (82/83 Soi 22, off Soi Ekamai) – and then the crowds died off. There could well be a second coming. Check for yourself by catching the Skytrain to Ekamai station.

🚌 air-con 6 🚹 Tha Banglamphu ⏰ 4pm-2am

Firecat (3, G7)

Firecat's menu of live shows sounded intriguing, a bit different from the rest – girl in champagne glass, midget on motorbike. But what could have been erotic and entertaining or theatrical and camp was tawdry and downright dull. The yawns and intent conversation between the many couples confirmed that we weren't the only ones to think so.

✉ **Soi Patpong 1, Silom** 🚉 **Sala Daeng** 🚌 air-con 2, 4, 5, 15 ⏰ 6pm-2am 💲 400B

The Oxygen Zone (3, C7)

You'd think selling oxygen to Bangkokians would be a cinch, but the Oxygen Zone wasn't exactly crowded with wheezing locals ordering a puff. Maybe it's the retirement home atmosphere of leather recliner lounge-chairs, tubes and oxygen masks. Nevertheless, it's still a peaceful, smoke-free spot for a drink.

✉ **2nd fl, Centrepoint shopping centre, Soi 3, Siam Sq** 🕿 **02 658 4822** 🚉 **Siam** 🚌 16, 21, 25, 40, 141 ⏰ 10am-10pm

Q Bar (3, C14)

Q Bar is well and truly Bangkok's 'it' bar. 'It' is where movie stars slouch into the dark padded-leather walls, socialites all but swing off the upstairs balcony so everyone can see them and serious lushes spend hours reading the

drinks menu, with 37 types of vodka.

✉ **34 Soi 11, Th Sukhumvit** 🕿 **02 252 3274** 🚉 **Nana** 🚌 air-con 1, 8 , 11, 13 ⏰ 8pm-2am 💲 400B Fri-Sat

Shenanigan's (3, H7)

Bangkok has been no more immune to the Irish pub cultural invasion than any other world city. But Shenanigan's has managed to make the formula seem genuine with live music and happy patrons. It's also one of the few places in this town that serve Guinness.

✉ **1/5-6 Th Convent, Silom** 🕿 **02 266 7160** 🚉 **Sala Daeng** 🚌 air-con 2, 4, 5, 15 ⏰ 11.30-2am

Tapas (3, G7)

Early in the night, this Moorish-style bar is mellow, with wavering candlelight on the rendered walls. Everyone lies back against big cushions, picking at tapas and nod-

Drinks are on cue at Q Bar.

ding to the chilled-out beats. Then later the disco ball starts swirling and the dancefloor gets sweaty at this Thai yuppie favourite.

✉ **114/7 Soi 4, Th Silom** 🕿 **02 632 0920** 🚉 **Sala Daeng** 🚌 air-con 2, 4, 5, 15 ⏰ 10pm-2am

Bangkok Beerfest

If you're around in November, December or January, look out for the open-air beerhalls that spring up outside some big shopping centres from 5pm every day – the beer's usually cheap and the music cheesy, but everyone sings along to it anyway. Try the World Trade Centre (3, B9) and the Amari Boulevard Hotel (3, D13).

DANCE CLUBS

Bangkok's dance clubs are the domain of young, rich, conspicuously consuming Thais. The city isn't exactly overloaded with clubs, probably because most people choose to drink and dance more cheaply at bars. The cover charge usually includes a drink.

Concept CM2 (3, C8)

This Siam Square club has its bases well and truly covered. There's something for everyone – covers bands belt out funky favourites, giggling gals pretend they're Janet Jackson at the karaoke machine and twinkle-toed types boogie the night away under the disco ball.
✉ **Novotel Bangkok on Siam Sq, Soi 6, Siam Sq** ☎ **02 255 6888** 🚇 **Siam** 🚌 **16, 21, 25, 40, 141** ⏰ 7pm–2am ⑤ **100B**

Lucifer (3, G7)

This is no burn-baby-burn disco inferno. Sure, there's a cute papier mâché devil at the entrance, but Lucifer is a serious club for hardcore techno. Ravers who used to dance all night here must be ruing the new early closing times.
✉ **2nd fl, Radio City, Soi Patpong 1, Th Silom**

Ministry of Sound

☎ **02 234 6902**
🚇 **Sala Daeng**
🚌 **air-con 2, 4, 5, 15**
⏰ 8pm–2am ⑤ **100B**

Ministry of Sound (3, E14)

We can forgive this kind of cultural imperialism. The Bangkok branch of the British überclub opened in early 2002 and is – are you sur-

prised? – far and away the best dance club in the city, with three floors, a neo-industrial fitout and the very best touring DJs.
✉ **4 Soi 12, Th Sukhumvit** ☎ **02 229 5888** 🚇 **Nana**
🚌 **air-con 1, 8 , 11, 13**
⏰ 10pm–2am ⑤ **500B**

Narcissus (4, B3)

Never has a club been so aptly named. It's mind-boggling to think of the amount of mirror-looking and breathless self-admiration that must have gone on before the designer-label-bedecked young things here could leave the house. But you can't begrudge this grandiose club its ability to pull the top DJs.
✉ **112 Soi 3, Th Sukhumvit** ☎ **02 258 4805** 🚇 **Asok**
⏰ 9pm–2am ⑤ **300B (incl 2 drinks), 500B (incl 3 drinks) Sat-Sun**

CINEMAS

Bangkok has dozens of cinemas screening movies in English, with Thai subtitles – check the listings mags for details. Tickets cost around 100B to 120B, with no discounts for kids, but the cultural centres often show movies for free. Banglamphu's 'cinemas' (read: eateries showing badly pirated videos) often have new releases before the cinemas.

Alliance Française
(3, J9) If you feel like intensity of a different nationality, check out the French movies (with English subtitles). Keep an eye on the Alliance Française website to see what's showing.
✉ **29 Th Sathon Tai, Silom** ☎ **02 670 4200** **e** **www.alliance-fran caise.or.th** 🚇 **Sala Daeng** 🚌 **air-con 15, 67** ♿

Goethe Institute
(3, H11) Expats and film buffs catch the regular screenings of German-language films and theme nights, like a Wim Winders retrospective, at this cultural centre. You don't have to speak German, as the films have English subtitles, and there's a great beer garden for a drink before, during or after a show.
✉ **18/1 Soi Goethe, Th Sathon Tai, Silom** ☎ **02 287 0726** 🚇 **Sala Daeng** 🚌 **air-con 15, 67** ♿

Grand EGV Gold Class (3, B7)
Place your snack order on the way in, wait until after the royal anthem to recline your sofa chair to horizontal and snuggle in for the long haul. Try not to fall asleep before your food arrives.
✉ **6th fl, Siam Discovery Centre, Th Ram I, Siam Sq**

Cinema Basics

Bangkok's cinemas are blissfully heat and humidity free. So much so that – you'll probably never be told this again in Bangkok – you should dress warmly so you don't shiver in the Arctic-level air-conditioning. The Thai royal anthem is played before every movie screening, so stand quietly and respectfully throughout.

☎ **02 658 0454** 🚇 **Siam** 🚌 **16, 21, 25, 40, 141** ⑤ **300B** ♿

SF Cinema City (3, C6)
Grab a big box of popcorn and find a seat among the Thai teenagers waiting to see the latest blockbuster. If that sounds like your worst nightmare, spend the extra cash and buy one of the gold-class seats (200B).
✉ **7th fl, Mah Boon Krong, cnr Th Phra Ram I & Th Phayathai, Siam Sq** ☎ **02 611 6444** 🚇 **National**

Stadium 🚌 **air-con 1, 2, 29, 141** ♿

UA Emporium (4, C3)
On the very top floor of the Emporium shopping centre, this cinema serves up the usual Hollywood shoot-and-snog standards. But this cinema stands out because of its fab sound and projection quality.
✉ **6th fl, The Emporium, btw Sois 22 & 24, Th Sukhumvit** ☎ **02 664 8711** 🚇 **Phrom Phong** 🚌 **air-con No 1, 2, 8, 11, 13, 38** ♿

ROCK, JAZZ & BLUES

If too much jazz is never enough, you could also slip in a meal at Fabb Fashion Café (3, C10) and Le Cafe Siam (3, J12) which have bands nightly, or Eat Me (3,H7), with live music streaming from its balcony every Thursday and Saturday.

Bamboo Bar (2, P9)

You could be forgiven for thinking that Thailand was actually colonised by the Brits when you visit the Bamboo Bar, the city's top jazz spot. Patrons sip G&Ts while lounging in leopard-skin chairs, feeling a million miles away from the heat and dust, while jazz bands or singers soothe any remaining tensions.

✉ **48 Soi Oriental, Th Charoen Krung, Bangrak** ☎ **02 236 0400** 🚇 **Saphan Taksin** 🚌 **75, 115, 116** ⛴ **Tha Oriental & hotel shuttle boat from Tha Sathon** ⊙ **Fri-Sat 11-2am, Sun-Thur 11-1am**

Jazzing it up at the Bamboo Bar.

The Living Room

(3, E15) We'll come clean straight up – the Living Room is a hotel buffet restaurant. But where most of its ilk are sedated by corny covers bands, this cosy upmarket place is alive with the grooves of some of the top jazz acts around. The mellow Sunday brunch starts around 11am.

✉ **250 Th Sukhumvit, btw Sois 12 & 14, Khlong Toey** ☎ **02 653 0333** 🚇 **Asok** 🚌 **air-con 1, 8 , 11, 13** ⊙ **10am-1pm**

Saxophone (1, F3)

Saxophone is still Bangkok's premier live music venue, a dark, intimate space where you can pull up a chair just a few metres away from the band and see their every bead of sweat. If you like some mystique in your musicians, watch the blues, jazz, reggae or rock from the balcony.

✉ **3/8 Th Phayathai, Victory Monument** ☎ **02 246 5472** 🚇 **Victory Monument** 🚌 **any bus heading north up Th Phayathai** ⊙ **6pm-2am**

The Soi Dogs in action at the Living Room

TRADITIONAL MUSIC, THEATRE & DANCE

There's a lot of very average, made-for-tourist music, theatre and dancing in Bangkok. So try to catch one of these highly regarded *khon* (masked drama), *lákhon* (traditional folk tales, often sung) or puppet performances.

Chalermkrung Royal Theatre (2, J5)

This restored Thai Deco building – originally known, as the sign outside indicates, as Sala Chaloem Krung – hosts traditional khon performances as well as modern Thai-language drama. Here khon is a high-tech production, with a flash audio system and computer-generated laser graphics. Dress respectfully (no shorts, sleeveless tops or sandals).

✉ cnr Th Charoen Krung & Th Triphet, Phahurat ☎ 02 222 0434 ᗑ air-con 1, 7, 8 ⛴ Tha Saphan Phut ⑤ 100B ♿

Interior detail, Chalermkrung Royal Theatre

Joe Louis Puppet Theatre (1, C2)

From his Nonthaburi workshop-cum-theatre, Joe

Traditional dance, Sala Rim Naam

Louis (aka Sakorn Yangkhiawsod) creates traditional Thai masks and puppets for the daily khon performances. The hike out there is worth it (especially if you have kids) for the exquisite craftmanship and entertaining shows, where each puppet is controlled by three people.

✉ 96/48 Moo 7, Soi Krungthep-Nonthaburi 12, Nonthaburi ☎ 02 527 7737-8 ⛴ Tha Nonthaburi, then take a taxi ⏲ mask production & show 9.30-11am, show Fri-Sat 7.30-9pm ⑤ B600 ♿

National Theatre (6, D2)

The National Theatre has kept the traditional khon dance-drama alive through its slumps in popularity. Originally only performed for the royal court, khon depicts scenes from the *Ramakian*, Thailand's version of India's *Ramayana*, and is a huge production involving hundreds of masked characters. You can also catch a lákhon show here, too.

✉ Th Ratchini, Ratanakosin ☎ 02 224 1342 ᗑ air-con 15, 39, 153 ⛴ Tha Phra Chan ⏲ Sat & Sun ⑤ 20-200B ♿

Sala Rim Naam (2, P8)

The riverside Sala Rim Naam – a stunning Thai pavilion made of teak, marble and bronze – holds nightly classical dance performances which are far superior to the average tourist fare. It's part of the Oriental Hotel (just across the river), so the meal is as classy as the show. Bookings recommended.

✉ Oriental Hotel, 48 Soi Oriental, Th Charoen Krung, Bangrak ☎ 02 437 2918 ⛴ free shuttle boat from Oriental Hotel ⏲ 7-10pm ⑤ 1600B ♿

GAY & LESBIAN BANGKOK

The Balcony (3, G7)

The Balcony is your classic all-round, good-time bar, where cute young boys in hotpants and string vests check out the talent on the street and tables of straight couples order rounds of the cheapest drinks around. A table outside under the red lanterns is the prime position for watching the passing parade.

⊠ Soi 4, Th Silom, Silom ☎ 02 235 5891
🚇 Sala Daeng
🚌 air-con 2, 4, 5, 15
⏲ until 2am

DJ Station (3, G8)

Neo-industrial DJ Station is the hottest gay dance club in town. The music varies wildly from handbag to hard house but the dance floor remains packed with shirtless sweaty boys. Avoid if you're claustrophobic or just hang out at the 3rd-floor chillout area.

⊠ 8/6-8 Soi 2, Th Silom ☎ 02 266 4029
🚇 Sala Daeng
🚌 air-con 2, 4, 5, 15
⏲ 10pm-2am ⑤ 100B Sun-Thur (incl 1 drink), 200B Fri-Sat (incl 2 drinks)

Brand with Wings

Once it was used by Thai wage slaves and truck drivers to pull them through their hellishly long hours at work. Then an Austrian entrepreneur bought the non-Asian marketing rights to this Kratieng Daeng drink, repackaged it for a clubbing crowd and the Red Bull phenomenon was born. In Bangkok, you can buy the original, which tastes a bit different to the Red Bull sold in the West, in little brown bottles with the familiar blue-and-white label.

Expresso (3, G8)

Expresso looks too cool for its own good, but don't take that as a bad thing in manic Soi 2. Its relative calm and sophistication is good news for those who can't take the noise and crowds of the big clubs. Lots of looking goes on through the floor-to-ceiling windows.

⊠ Soi 2, Th Silom, Silom ☎ 02 632 7223
🚇 Sala Daeng
🚌 air-con 2, 4, 5, 15
⏲ 6pm-2am

Happen (3, G8)

Happen is a mellow, friendly little bar that most guys use as a pitstop before hitting the dance clubs. Many often return – after getting sick of the sweat, crowds

and hardcore music – to dance to more relaxed beats or give the karaoke machine a workout.

⊠ 8/14 Soi 2, Th Silom ☎ 02 235 2552
🚇 Sala Daeng
🚌 air-con 2, 4, 5, 15
⏲ 8pm-2am

JJ Park (3, G8)

If dance and techno is not your thing but high camp is, drop by JJ Park for its fabulous drag shows. It may be on Soi 2 but the crowd is usually completely different to the standard. Regulars also recommend the live music and comedy shows.

⊠ 8/3 Soi 2, Th Silom ☎ 02 233 3247
🚇 Sala Daeng
🚌 air-con 2, 4, 5, 15
⏲ 10pm-2am

Telephone (3, G7)

Muscle boys and queens parade past Telephone's outdoor tables, taking in the scene at one of Bangkok's oldest and most popular gay bars. Inside, all the tables have a telephone you can use to call any patrons you fancy.

⊠ 114/11-13 Soi 4, Th Silom, Silom ☎ 02 234 3279 🚇 Sala Daeng
🚌 air-con 2, 4, 5, 15
⏲ until 2am

Watch the world go by at The Balcony.

SPECTATOR SPORT

Bangkokians are not the most sporty of people (bit hard, considering the lack of recreation space) but they do have their favourite spectator sports.

For two Sundays a month, the **Royal Bangkok Sports Club** (3, D8; 1 Th Henri Dunant, Pathumwan; ☎ 02-251 0181-86; 🚇 Ratchadamri) is a frenzy of furious betting, drinking and horse-racing. Usually the domain of members (and there is a whopping waiting list), the club opens its doors to the great unwashed for the races. The other main racing venue is the **Royal Turf Club** (2, D9; 183 Th Phitsanulok, Dusit, ☎ 02 280 0020-5; 🚌 air-con 9), not far from Chitlada Palace. It hosts Bangkok's biggest horse race, the King's Cup, around the first or second week of January as well as regular races on alternate Sundays to the RBSC.

Maybe Bangkok's passion for soccer stems from the old Siamese football, or *takraw*. Players usually stand around in a circle and kick a woven rattan ball soccer-style, trying to keep it airborne and earning points for the style, difficulty and variety of their kicking manoeuvres. In international competition (the Thais introduced the sport to the South-East Asian Games and, with the Malaysians, have dominated it) *takraw* is played like volleyball, except only the feet and head may touch the ball. There aren't that many regular professional games played, but go to Lumphini Park and you'll probably see an impromptu match.

The most dynamic and exciting Thai sport is muay thai, or Thai boxing, considered by many to be the ultimate in hand-to-hand fighting. Matches can be violent, but the surrounding spectacle of crazy music, pre-match rituals and manic betting is worth the ticket price alone.

> ### It's Got a Ring to It
> When a Thai boxer is ready for the ring, he is given a new name to fight under – usually a none-too-subtle reminder of how much pain these guys aim to inflict. Just so you know what you might be in for, a recent session at Lumphini stadium boasted clashes like: Dangerous Uneven-Legged Man vs The Bloody Elbow, The Human Stone vs The King of the Knee and No Mercy Killer vs The Golden Left Leg.

Fights are held at **Ratchadamnoen Boxing Stadium** (2, E7; Th Ratchadamnoen Nok, btw Th Krung Kasem & Th Chakkaphatdi, Dusit; ☎ 02 281 4205; 🚌 air-con 3, 9) and **Lumphini Boxing Stadium** (3, H11; Th Rama IV, btw Th Withayu & Expressway, Lumphini; ☎ 02 251 4303; 🚌 air-con 7, 141). Ratchadamnoen fights are on Monday and Wednesday at 6pm, Thursday at 5pm and 9pm, and Sunday at 6pm, while Lumphini hosts them on Tuesday and Friday at 6.30pm and Saturday at 5pm and 8.30pm. Tickets cost either 230B, 460B or 1000B (ringside) – ignore the touts, always buy from the ticket windows and don't believe anyone, except a window ticket-vendor, that says seats are sold out.

THE SEX INDUSTRY

You wouldn't pick that prostitution is illegal in Thailand. Nor would you guess that most of its sex workers exist for Thais, not the foreigners that crowd the go-go bars of Patpong, Thaniya, Nana Entertainment Plaza and Soi Cowboy. But just as appearances can be deceiving, the mythology of Bangkok's sex industry – as a Western-dominated sleazefest established by American GIs – doesn't quite match its history.

Like Indians, Thai men for centuries took concubines. It was perfectly okay for them to keep several mistresses, as it still is for high-ranking men today. Chinese immigrants set up brothels in Chinatown's notorious Sampeng Lane in the mid-19th century – and these later expanded throughout the country. Prostitution was finally declared illegal in the 1950s but just decades later, as the Vietnam War brought Western men to Bangkok for R&R, a new era of prostitutes catering for foreigners began. The city's first massage parlour opened in Soi Thaniya for Japanese expats (still the soi's biggest customers today) and Thai police officials. The Patpong area, just a few streets west on Soi Patpong 1 and 2, was originally a banana plantation and became a bar area to cater for nearby airline workers. It earned notoriety during the 1980s for its wild sex shows, involving everything from ping-pong balls to razors to midgets on motorbikes.

Today, Soi Cowboy and Nana Entertainment Plaza are the sleazier scenes, while Patpong seems an almost family-friendly affair. Grandparents stroll hand-in-hand and casually look into go-go bars, and the audiences in sex shows are often dominated by couples, rather than drunken men. But most sex-show visitors are still getting ripped off through various scams while the women performing – mostly from poor areas of Bangkok looking to make their fortune, escape abuse or subsidise their family's meagre income – are at high risk of drug addiction and sexually transmitted diseases.

Strip clubs along Soi Patpong 1

places to stay

Bangkok has always known how to look after its visitors. Last century, the Oriental Hotel was the home-away-from-home of choice for adventurous artists and writers, like Somerset Maugham who spent months there recovering from a bout of malaria. During and after the Vietnam War, American soldiers R&R'd in hotels named after cities back home like Reno and Miami, while travellers on the overland hippy trail crashed at guesthouses around Soi Ngam Duphli.

These days, visitors are more likely to hit the sack in the famous backpackers ghetto of Banglamphu or live it up on a package holiday to luxury hotels with a giddying number of rooms and facilities, like world-class restaurants, and an incredible service ethic. But many are turning to the smaller, more intimate boutique hotels that have sprung up in the Silom area.

Room Rates

The categories indicate the cost per night of a standard double room, including all tax and service charges, during the high season.

Deluxe	over 8000B
Top End	5000-7999B
Mid-Range	1000-4999B
Budget	under 999B

If there's one legacy of the Asian economic boom, besides empty apartment blocks, it's the business focus of the top-end and deluxe hotels. Even a room that appears to be a temple to relaxation will have a desk and facilities like direct-dial phones and modem connections. It's rare for one of these hotels not to have a top-notch business centre.

Business travellers tend to stay in the white-collar districts of Silom and Sukhumvit, also favoured by lone male travellers for their proximity to 'entertainment' districts like Patpong, Nana Entertainment Plaza and Soi Cowboy. Siam Square, Silom and Sukhumvit are convenient for shopaholics, foodies and barflies. If you want to see the sights or live cheaply, you're probably better off making a camp in Banglamphu – many of the must-sees are within walking or boating distance, though the Skytrain connection to the river express has made these sights more accessible. Banglamphu is a peaceful, riverside area which hasn't sacrificed its old buildings to high-rises.

Facade of the luxurious Marriott in Sukhumvit

DELUXE

Banyan Tree (3, J9)
This little sister of the legendary Phuket retreat is the most touchy-feely of Bangkok's deluxe hotels, where oil-burner scents and new age music blend seamlessly with the sleek modern Asian design. Skip the tiny pool and head for the sanctuary of your suite or the day spa (p. 47).
✉ **21/100 Th Sathorn Tai, Silom** ☎ **02 679 1200; fax 679 1199** e **www.banyantree .com** 🚇 **Sala Daeng** 🚌 **air-con 15, 67** ✕ **Bai Yun**

Grand Hyatt Erawan

Grand Hyatt Erawan (3, C9) Every room in this imposing neoclassical edifice is an art gallery, right down to the originals in your suite's loo. But that's just one bonus of staying here: what about the shopping centres just a credit-card swipe away?
✉ **cnr Th Ratchadamri & Th Ploenchit** ☎ **02 254 1234; fax 02 254 6308** e **bangkok. hyatt.com/bangh** 🚇 **Chitlom** 🚌 **air-con 4, 5, 15** ✕ **Dining Room**

Oriental Hotel (2, P9)
The Sir James A Michener suite gives an inkling of why this establishment is one of the world's most famous hotels. Sir James liked his writing desk overlooking the river and an enormous red claw-foot bath which is the highlight of the bathroom — testament to the Oriental's enduring philosophies of timeless style and service above and beyond the call of duty.
✉ **48 Soi Oriental, Th Charoen Krung,**

Bangrak ☎ **02 236 0400; fax 2659 0000** e **reserve-orbkk@ mohg.com; www.man darinoriental.com** 🚇 **Saphan Taksin** 🚌 **75, 115, 116** ⛴ **Tha Oriental & hotel shuttle boat from Tha Sathorn** ✕ **Le Normandie (p. 88)**

Peninsula Hotel (3, J1)
This new kid on Bangkok's luxury block — and sister of Hong Kong's legendary Peninsula — has sweeping views from a rare vantage point, Thonburi. While it might lack the Oriental's classic appeal, it more than makes up for it with modern toys such as bathroom televisions featuring condensation-free screens, a 60m swimming pool and a helipad.
✉ **333 Th Charoen Nakhon, Thonburi** ☎ **02 861 2888; fax 861 1112** e **pbk@pen insula.com; www.penin sula.com** ⛴ **hotel shuttle boat from Tha Sathorn** ✕ **Mei Jiang (p. 88)**

Peninsula Hotel

Regent Bangkok

(3, D9) Service is the undoubted cornerstone of the Regent experience. Worried about trying to get to meetings on time without getting stuck in traffic? Use the hotel's office on wheels, where you can work away completely oblivious to the surrounding gridlock. And olde-worlde style comes just as effortlessly – just try high tea in the lobby, complete with a string quartet.

✉ 155 Th Ratchadamri ☎ 02 251 6127; fax 251 5390
🖳 www.regent hotels.com
🚈 Ratchadamri
🚌 air-con 4, 5, 15
🍴 Regent Lobby (p. 88)

Shangri-La Hotel

(3, J2) The firmly family-friendly Shangri-La had long been one of the world's top hotels when it built the glamorous Krung Thep wing, where the rooms open onto a spacious balcony overflowing with magenta bougainvillea and, if they're west-facing, a lofty river vista. Now, the competition is tougher than ever.

✉ 89 Soi Wat Suan Plu, Th Charoen Krung, Bangrak
☎ 02 236 7777; fax 236 8579
🖳 slbk@shangri-la .com; www.shangri-la .com 🚈 Saphan Taksin
🚤 Tha Sathon
🚌 75, 115, 116
🍴 Angelini (p. 87)
♿

The world-renowned Shangri-La Hotel

Chain Hotel Booking Lines

If you're planning to stay in a hotel that's part of a chain, it might be easier to book it in your home country by calling these numbers (all are toll-free unless otherwise noted).

Amari 1800 221 176 (Australia), 0990 300 220 (UK toll call), 1-800-44 UTELL (USA)

Hyatt 131 234 (Australia), 020-8335 1220 (UK toll call), 888 591 1234 (USA)

Mandarin Oriental 1800 123 693 (Australia), 49-69 66 419 712 (UK toll call), 800 526 6566 (USA & Canada)

Marriott 1800 251 259 (Australia), 0800 221222 (UK), 1888 236 2427 (USA & Canada)

Shangri-La 1800 222 448 (Australia), 020-8747 8485 (UK toll call), 1800 942 5050 (USA)

Sheraton 1800 073 535 (Australia), 00 800 325 35353 (UK), 00 800 325 3535 (USA & Canada)

Small Luxury Hotels (Banyan Tree) 1800 251 958 (Australia), 00 800 525 48000 (UK), 800 525 4800 (USA & Canada)

Summit Hotels & Resorts (Landmark) 1800 801 855 (Australia), 0800 556 555 (UK), 1800 457 400 (USA & Canada)

Sheraton Grande Sukhumvit (3, E15)

Decisions, decisions. Do you recline thoughtfully on cushions in the shade of a poolside sala, check into the dark and intimate day spa-to-die-for (p. 47) or snap your fingers to world-class jazz on offer in the Living Room bar (p. 96)? High-class relaxation can be tough.

✉ 250 Th Sukhumvit, btw Sois 12 & 14, Khlong Toey ☎ 02 653 0333; fax 653 0400
🖳 grande.sukhumvit@ luxurycollection.com; www.luxurycollection .com/grandesukhumvit
🚈 Asok 🚌 air-con 1, 8, 11, 13 🍴 bars, cafes & restaurants, including basil (p. 80) and the Living Room ♿

TOP END

Amari Airport Hotel
(1, G3) The rooms are tired and overpriced but you can't beat the location, location, location. Geared specifically towards the transit traveller, who can book in for a 3hr ministay or watch departure and arrival schedules on TV, this hotel is an easy stumble across a walkway from the international airport.
✉ 333 Th Chert Wudthakas (enter via walkway from terminal 1) ☎ 02 566 1020; fax 566 1941 e airport@amari.com; www.amari.com 🚉 suburban train to Don Muang 🚌 air-con 4, 10, 13, 29; air-port bus A-1, A-2, A-3, A-4 ✗ Taurus Brew-house (p. 89) ♿

Amari Watergate Hotel (3, A9)
As you'd expect of a flag-ship hotel, the Watergate is a sophisticated embodi-ment of all that the home-grown Amari chain stands for: good management, Thai-inspired design, friendly service and a will-ingness to go the extra yards to cater for families

Baiyoke Sky Hotel

and disabled travellers.
✉ 847 Th Phetburi, Pratunam ☎ 02 653 9000; fax 653 9045 e reservations@watergate.amari.com 🚌 air-con 5, 11, 12 🚤 river taxi to Nailert ✗ Grappino (p. 83) ♿

Baiyoke Sky Hotel
(1, G3) You can't miss the main attraction here: every-thing, including the 84th floor, revolves around the view from Thailand's tallest

tower. Your vantage point, in the heart of Pratunam, will come in handy when planning your traffic-defying strategies.
✉ 222 Th Ratchaprarop, Pratunam ☎ 02 656 3000; fax 656 3555 e baiyoke@mozart.inet.co.th; www.baiyokehotels.co.th 🚌 air-con 4, 13, 15, 38, 139, 140 ✗ Bangkok Sky Restaurant

Bangkok Marriott Resort & Spa (1, H1)
Set amid the lushest land-scaped gardens by the river, the Marriott really is that cliched place where you can get away from it all – home, hassles and even Bangkok. You can either laze about the divine poolside area or indulge in a Manohra Rice Barge Dinner Cruise (p. 56).
✉ 257 Th Charoen Nakhon, Thonburi ☎ 02 476 0022; fax 476 1120 e www.marriotthotels.com/bkkth 🚤 hotel shuttle boat from Tha Sathorn, Tha Oriental & Tha River City ♿

The Landmark Bangkok (3, D13)
The revolving entry door here hasn't stopped turn-ing with working travellers, thanks to a business centre that never sleeps and staff who understand corporate culture. But now with the Skytrain only a 3min walk away, package holiday-makers are starting to appreciate the luxuriously practical Landmark.
✉ 138 Th Sukhumvit

The Swiss Lodge is ideal for fondue aficionados.

Boom, Boom, Boom? Not in my Room!

As you've no doubt noticed, the sex industry permeates every aspect of Bangkok tourism. Some middle-of-the-road hotels, like the Grace Hotel in Little Arabia and many places along Th Silom, are notorious for offering guests, especially solo men, service with an extra smile (and slap and tickle). So if you don't want to be continually asked if you want a massage or company, nor want to be kept awake by other guests' nocturnal adventures, query your prospective hotel about their policy.

(btw Sois 4 & 6) ☎ 02 254 0404; fax 253 4259 e email@landmark bangkok.com; www .landmarkbangkok.com 🚇 Nana 🚌 air-con 1, 8, 11, 13 🍽 Nipa Thai

Novotel Bangkok on Siam (3, C8)

The Novotel is in a nifty position if you're in Bangkok for the shopping. It's located within walking or Skytraining distance of the big centres, like MBK and the World Trade Centre, and is one of the cheapest top-end options available.
✉ Soi 6, Siam Sq

☎ 02 255 6888; fax 255 1824 e reserve@ novotelbkk.com; www .novotel.co.th/siam 🚇 Siam 🚌 16, 21, 25, 40, 141

The Swiss Lodge (3, H7)

Don't be fooled by the name – there's not a cuckoo clock in sight at this classy boutique hotel situated in the heart of the Silom district. With only 57 rooms, it is a quiet, well-managed option for both business-people and couples. However, Swiss kitsch aficionados shouldn't despair: fondue is a speciality of the inhouse restaurant.
✉ 3 Th Convent, Silom ☎ 02 233 5345; fax 236 9425 e info@ swisslodge.com; www .swisslodge.com 🚇 Sala Daeng 🚌 air-con 2, 4, 5, 15 🍽 Café Swiss

Sukhothai Hotel (3, H9)

Designed by Edward Tuttle, the creative hand behind Phuket's heavenly Amanpuri resort, the Sukhothai is a low-rise temple to Asian minimalism. Sukhothai-era-inspired artworks in the rooms, around the expansive gardens and in the still ponds are constant reminders of Tuttle's inspiration – Thailand's first kingdom of Sukhothai.
✉ 13/3 Th Sathon Tai, Silom ☎ 02 287 0222; fax 287 4980 e info@ sukhothai.com; www .sukhothai.com 🚇 Sala Daeng 🚌 air-con 15, 67 🍽 Celadon (p. 85)

Small stupas decorate the pool at the Sukhothai Hotel.

MID-RANGE

Bangkok Christian Guesthouse (3, H8)

A Christian guesthouse just a short stroll from the sex-for-sale strips of Patpong and Thaniya? Yes, somewhat incongruous, but this place's many fans like its atmosphere of calm amid the craziness. Set in a big garden, it will be an excellent option when it reopens in late-2002 after a spruce-up.

✉ **123 Soi 2, Th Convent, Silom ☎ 02 233 6303; fax 237 1742** 📧 **bcgh@loxinfo.co.th** 🚇 **Sala Daeng** 🚌 **air-con 2, 4, 5, 15**

Grand Inn (3, C13)

The Grand Inn is in the thick of Little Arabia, a fascinating area that's alive at all hours of the day and night. It's a small little hotel, with friendly staff and well-maintained rooms with all the facilities. The Skytrain's only a 5min walk away.

✉ **2/7-8 Soi 3 (Nana), Th Sukhumvit, Pathumwan ☎ 02 254 9021-5; fax 254 9020** 🚇 **Nana** 🚌 **air-con 1, 8, 11, 13** ⚥

Jim's Lodge (3, E12)

Jim's is a small, comfortable hotel situated in an embassy and expat residential area not far from Lumphini Park. Families will find it all-too-easy to colonise the suites with a lounge and kitchen area, while lounge lizards can soak up the sun and bubbles of the roof-top terrace and spa.

✉ **125/7 Soi Ruam Rudi, Th Ploenchit, Pathumwan**

Royal Hotel

☎ **02 255 3100; fax 253 8492** 📧 **jimslodge@yahoo .com** 🚇 **Ploenchit** 🚌 **air-con 1, 8, 11, 13** ⚥

La Résidence Hotel & Serviced Apartments (3, H5)

Another sign of the changing face of Bangkok's accommodation scene, La Résidence is a relatively new boutique hotel not far from the Silom scene. The 26 rooms are bright, cheerful and modern (the suites on the top floor with a balcony are especially tasteful) and can be rented by the month.

✉ **173/8-9 Th Surawong ☎ 02 266 5400; fax 237 9322** 📧 **residence@loxinfo .co.th** 🚇 **Chong Nonsi** 🚌 **1, 16, 35, 36, 75, 93**

Majestic Suites (3, D13)

Majestic seems too grand a name for such an intimate hotel with stylish rooms and top-notch security. But the location – a step off Th Sukhumvit

and a stroll from the Skytrain – is certainly princely.

✉ **110-110/1 Th Sukhumvit (btw Sois 4 & 6), Pathumwan ☎ 02 656 8220; fax 656 8201** 📧 **aman@ majesticsuites.com; www.majesticsuites .com** 🚇 **Nana** 🚌 **air-con 1, 8, 11, 13**

New Trocadero (3, H3)

It's a pity about the New Trocadero's location in the shade of the Phayathai-Bangkhlo Expressway because it's a reliable mid-range choice, especially considering its recent renovation, big swimming pool and closeness to Th Silom and the river. There are some good eateries located nearby, catering for the African and Arab travellers who stay here.

✉ **34 Th Surawong, Bangrak ☎ 02 234 8920-8; fax 234 8929** 📧 **newtroc@ksc.th .com** 🚌 **air-con 4, 5, 15** ⚓ **Tha Oriental**

Royal Hotel (6, E3)

An old Bangkok faithful with a marble lobby that echoes with muzak tinkles, the Royal is a handy jumping-off point for a Ratanakosin ramble, temple crawl or just a laze around Sanam Luang. Most taxi drivers know it as 'the Ratanakosin'.

✉ **cnr Th Ratchadam-noen Klang & Th Atsadang, Banglamphu ☎ 02 222 9111; fax 224 2083** 🚌 **air-con 2, 3, 6, 9, 11, 12, 15, 17, 39, 44, 68, 153** ✖ **Royal Hotel Coffee Shop**

Viengtai (6, D4)

The Viengtai is all cool, marbled reticence surrounded by the Khao San madness. The ice princess attitude also extends to the staff, but if you don't let that bother you, you'll realise that you're in sheer comfort in one of the best locations in Banglamphu.

✉ **42 Th Tani (main entry on Th Rambutri), Banglamphu** ☎ **02 280 5434; fax 281 8153** **e** **info@viengtai.co .th; www.viengtai.co.th** 🚐 **air-con 6, 17** 🚢 **Tha Banglamphu**

Staying for a While?

Most serviced apartments are ridiculously priced because they cater for the Western expat whose company blindly picks up the tab. A good alternative is to negotiate month-long rates at hotels like La Résidence Hotel & Serviced Apartments, Jim's Lodge and the Swiss Lodge.

White Orchid Hotel

(2, K8) Smack-bang in the middle of the Chinatown action, this hotel's rooms are clean and good-value. Combine that with its Cantonese restaurant and you'll understand why this venue is popular with Chinese visitors. Only prob-

lem is, it can be a nightmare trying to explore other areas of Bangkok from here.

✉ **409-21 Th Yaowarat, Chinatown** ☎ **02 226 0026; fax 225 6403** 🚐 **air-con 1, 7** 🚢 **Tha Ratchawong** ✗ **White Orchid Restaurant (p. 79)**

BUDGET

The Atlanta (3, E13)

Every city needs a place like the Atlanta, where the important things in life haven't changed since the 1950s. Classical music and jazz stream from the sound system, letter-writing desks come equipped with fans and film classics screen nightly. Go for the fan-cooled rooms on floors A and B.

✉ **78 Soi 2, Th Sukhumvit, Pratunam** ☎ **02 252 6069; fax 656 8123** **e** **www.the atlantahotel.bizland.com** 🚇 **Nana** 🚐 **air-con 1, 8 , 11, 13** ✗ **The Atlanta Coffee Shop (p. 80)**

Miami (3, D14)

Miami is yet another Vietnam-era hotel named after an American city. It's looking its age (you could be forgiven for thinking you're in a 1970s American diner at the Paris Restaurant) but is popular with travellers wanting to

avoid Banglamphu and enjoy lounging around the kitsch pool.

✉ **2 Soi 13, Th Sukhumvit** ☎ **02 253 5611-3; fax 02 253 1266** **e** **miamihotel@ thaimail.com; mem bers.tripod.com/~miami hotel/** 🚇 **Nana** 🚐 **air-con 1, 8 , 11, 13**

New Siam Guesthouse II (6, C2)

Rooms at this brand-spanking new guesthouse, not far from the

Banglamphu river express pier, are good value. Unsurprisingly, it's popular with backpackers, who also crowd its sister hotel on Soi Chana Songkhram which boasts the same good security, reasonable prices and effective management.

✉ **50 Trok Rong Mahai, Th Phra Athit, Banglamphu** ☎ **02 282 2795; fax 629 0101** **e** **www.newsiam.net** 🚐 **air-con 6** 🚢 **Tha Banglamphu** ✗ **cafe**

Looking over the balcony to the pool, Miami Hotel.

Niagara (3, J6)
Tucked away in a small, quiet street not far back from Th Silom, Niagara is plain but amazingly good value. The halls might seem a little institutional, however, for a modest price you get clean rooms with a TV, bathroom and air-conditioning.

⊠ 26 Soi Seuksa Withaya, Th Silom
☎ 02 233 5783-4
🚇 Chong Nonsi
🚌 air-con 15, 67

Pra Arthit Mansion
(6, C2) It was called the Beerhostel, the owner said, but because it's gone luxurious, it's now got a fancy name. Luxury might be stretching it but its spacious rooms are better than most around here, not to mention on the doorstep of buzzing Th Phra Athit. No proper after-hours reception, though.

⊠ 22 Th Phra Athit, Banglamphu ☎ 02 280 0744; fax 280 0742
🖂 praarthit@hotmail .com 🚌 air-con 6
⚓ Tha Banglamphu
✕ Ricky's Coffee Shop (p. 77)

Reno Hotel (3, B6)
This Vietnam War veteran is now an R&R option for the

new millennium, where you can rest in simple rooms and recreate beside the pool. The newly licked-with-paint Reno is down a quiet soi lined with guesthouses, but is only a short walk away from the Skytrain and Siam Square shopping arcades.

⊠ 40 Soi Kasem San 1, Th Phra Ram I, Siam Sq ☎ 02 215 0026-7; fax 215 3430 🖂 reno hotel@clickta.com
🚇 National Stadium
⚓ canal taxi to Ratchathewi 🚌 air-con 8 ✕ Sorn's

Ryn's Cafe 'n Bed
(3, H8) This bright and modern B&B is a breath of fresh air (and that's saying

something in smoggy Bangkok). Down the road from the thriving Th Convent scene, Ryn's offers something for all budget travellers – from dorm beds to private doubles to a family room – and even a classy cafe.

⊠ 44/17 Th Convent, Silom ☎ 02 632 1323-7; fax 632 1323
🖂 ryns@hotmail.com; www.cafeandbed.com
🚇 Sala Daeng
🚌 air-con 15, 67
✕ Ryn's Cafe ♿

Sala Thai Daily Mansion (3, J12)
If there's the slightest sniff of a breeze around, you'll pick it up on the roof-top terrace here. And it's nice to see a budget place take pride in its interior decorating. This 'mansion' is in the Soi Ngam Duphli area, popular with budget travellers throughout the 1970s and 80s.

⊠ 15 Soi Saphan Khu (on a laneway just off this soi) ☎ 02 287 1436 🚌 air-con 7, 141

YWCA Bangkok International House
(3, H10) As you'd expect, this is a clean, simple and wholesome option. The rooms are well-appointed and you won't be turned away if you've got a Y chromosome. But to reach the Silom shopping, Skytrain and nightlife you'll have to hike across two hellishly busy major roads.

⊠ 13 Th Sathorn Tai, Silom ☎ 02 679 1280-4; fax 6791280
🖂 ywca@bangkok .com; www.thai.net /ywca 🚇 Sala Daeng
🚌 air-con 15, 67

Travelling with Children
It's a rare Bangkok hotel – but there are a few – that doesn't like hosting children. Even at the fanciest hotels, you'll probably find it hard to stop the staff playing with your kids. At most mid-range, top-end and deluxe hotels, you should have no problems organising a babysitter or finding somewhere for the kids to play. Budget hotels can be difficult if you have very little ones because the rooms are often small and noisy, and the facilities are limited and cramped. Most places will let kids under 12 stay in your room for free.

facts for the visitor

ARRIVAL & DEPARTURE

Bangkok is a major travel hub, so it has plenty of direct flights from capital cities in Asia, Australia, Canada, Continental Europe, the UK and USA.

This also means it's a good place to pick up a cheap airfare. Bus and train services to South-East Asian countries are not so reliable, direct or fast.

Air

Bangkok International Airport is in Don Muang, north of Bangkok, but it will be replaced by a bigger airport at Nong Ngu Hao, 20km east of the city, in 2004, if everything goes to plan.

Don Muang, as it's known, has excellent facilities, including its own brewhouse, banks, exchange counters, post office, Internet terminals and, in the transit lounge, day rooms with toilet facilities for hire. The small domestic terminal is connected to the international terminals by a covered walkway or you can catch the free shuttle bus.

Bangkok International Airport
Left Luggage

There's a 24hr left-luggage service in the hall connecting the two international terminals on the check-in floor – it charges 70B for 24hrs and 35B for every 12hrs afterwards.

Information
General Inquiries
☎ 02 535 1111 (international)
☎ 02 535 1253 (domestic)

Flight Information
international flights:
☎ 02 535 1254 (departures)
☎ 02 535 1301 (arrivals)

domestic flights:
☎ 02 535 1192 (departures)
☎ 02 535 1253 (arrivals)

Hotel Booking Service
The Thai Hotels Association booths in the arrivals halls can book accommodation for you, a process which can sometimes be complicated by the commissions they receive from hotels.

Airport Access
Train From Don Muang train station, just opposite the Amari Airport Hotel, regular trains run to Bangkok from around 5am to 8pm. A ticket to the main train station, Hualamphong, costs 5B on the regular and commuter trains, between 45B and 65B on the rapid or express trains; this trip takes around 45mins but it can take a while getting from Hualamphong to areas like Sukhumvit.

Bus There are plenty of bus services, both public and private, to central Bangkok and they leave regularly between 6am and midnight. The best is the airport express (100B), which runs every 15mins from 6am to midnight. The A-1 express runs from the Silom district, A-2 from Banglamphu, A-3 from Th Sukhumvit and A-4 from Hualamphong and Siam Square. Public buses take longer and won't allow you to take luggage – buses 29 and 59 and air-con buses 4, 10, 13 and 29 make the trip.

Taxi Ignore the taxi touts who might approach you in the arrivals hall and instead head for the metered taxi desk just outside. Someone will record your destination on a sheet of paper, which you should show to the driver but not give to them (if you are unhappy with your service, call the number on the paper and register a formal complaint).

A taxi trip into central Bangkok should cost around 150B to 250B, plus tolls and a 50B airport fee. Don't be shy in telling the driver to put the meter on – some drivers don't and then try to negotiate a fare.

Bus

Not for the faint-hearted, government and private buses do trips from Bangkok to towns and cities around Thailand, as well as to Malaysia.

Government buses tend to be more reliable; the better private buses leave from the three official terminals, instead of hotels or guesthouses.

Northern and northeastern services leave from the northern bus terminal (1, E3), buses to eastern destinations leave from the eastern bus terminal (1, H4) and buses to the south leave from the southern terminal (1, F1). Private buses can be booked through hotels, travel agencies or bus offices.

Train

Regional Trains

Train is the best way of exploring Thailand, as it's inexpensive, reliable and reasonably efficient. Bangkok has two main train terminals: Hualamphong (2, L10), near Chinatown, from which most long-distance trains leave, and Bangkok Noi (2, E1), in Thonburi, which looks after many commuter and short-line train routes, including Kanchanaburi.

Fare and timetable information is available at these stations. Trains come in three classes – 3rd-class seats can be hard on the bottom on a long trip.

Eastern & Oriental Express

Finally, an Orient express that actually starts in the Orient! This luxury train travels from Singapore to Bangkok and then to Chiang Mai. For information visit the website at e www.orient-express.com.

Travel Documents

Passport

To enter Thailand, your passport must be valid for six months from the date of entry.

Visas

Residents of Australia, Canada, New Zealand, the UK and USA can stay in Bangkok for 30 days without a visa, while South Africans can stay for 90 days.

If you plan on a longer trip, you should get a 60-day tourist visa or a 90-day non-immigrant visa before you leave.

Return/Onward Ticket

Technically, you're supposed to be able to demonstrate proof of a return or onward ticket, however, you are unlikely to be asked to show it.

Customs

You can't bring in illegal drugs, firearms or pornography.

Duty Free

Visitors can bring 1L of wine or spirits, 200 cigarettes or 250g of other smoking material without paying duty.

Departure Tax

International travellers have to pay a 500B departure tax before going through customs, while domestic travellers pay a 30B departure tax in the price of their ticket.

GETTING AROUND

Bangkok's congested traffic and the weather will dominate your decisions about city travel. It can be tricky deciphering Thai addresses. A *thanon* is a street, a *soi* a laneway that runs off a bigger street and a *tràwk* is an alley. So Soi 6, Th Sukhumvit, is the sixth street to run off Th Sukhumvit. Some sois are so big they are sometimes called both a soi and a thanon. Formal addresses often have confusing slashes and dashes, like 325/7-8 Th Charoen Krung. This stems from an old system of allocating property and means that numbers along a street don't always run consecutively.

Travel Passes

Skytrain's three-day tourist pass (280B) with unlimited trips is good value for more than 10 trips; otherwise opt for the 250/160B (adult/student; including 30B refundable deposit) 10-ride pass. There are also 15-trip (330/210B, including deposit) and 30-trip (540/360B) passes that, like the 250B pass, must be used within a month.

Bus

Public buses are cheap and regular, but restricted by traffic flow. Most lines run between 5am and 11pm, but there is a cream-and-red night bus on some routes. There are three types of bus (in various colours): regular buses, which charge between 2B and 10B per trip; air-con buses, which charge between 6B and 16B; and microbuses, where fares are a flat 25B and you are guaranteed a seat. If you plan on catching lots of buses, invest in a bus map – Nelles Maps' *Bangkok & Greater Bangkok* and the *Tour 'n' Guide Map to Bangkok Thailand* show routes.

Train

Skytrain

Since its virgin voyage in 1999, the Skytrain has revolutionised travel in some areas of Bangkok. It's a cool, quick and efficient way of getting to areas like Sukhumvit, Silom, Siam Square, Chatuchak, Victory Monument and Bangrak, and there are plans to expand it farther north, east and west. Trains arrive every few minutes from 6am to midnight.

Tickets cost between 10B and 40B, and are available from coin-only machines (get change from the office). The offices at each stop sell travel passes and multi-trip tickets (see Travel Passes earlier). Free shuttle buses on particular routes can drop you at Skytrain stations – see **e** www.bts.co.th for routes – and run from 6.30am to 10.30pm; you need a coupon, given when you buy a travel pass.

Suburban Trains

You're unlikely to use the train services that stop at some Bangkok stops on their way to regional Thailand, except perhaps to the airport.

Subway

Bangkok's first subway is being built and is supposed to be finished by the end of 2003, but 2004 is looking like a more likely date. Its route will include Hualamphong train station and stops along Th Phra Ram IV and Soi Asoke (21), Th Sukhumvit.

Boat

Chao Phraya River Express

Catching one of the Chao Phraya River Express boats that ply up and down the river, from Wat Ratchasingkhon in the south to Nonthaburi in the north, is one of the most fun and relaxing, though crowded, ways of getting around. The service runs from around 6am to 7.30pm – there's usually a boat every 10mins – and you can buy tickets (6B to 25B) on board. Boats with yellow or red-and-orange flags are expresses, running during peak times, and so don't make every stop.

Canal Taxis
Longtail taxis zip around the Bangkok *khlongs*, making quick but sometimes smelly trips along polluted waterways. Stops are usually under bridges and fares are a few baht. Your most likely route is along Khlong Saen Saep to Th Ratchadamri (Pratunam market and World Trade Centre), Th Ratchathewi (Jim Thompson's House and Siam Square) and Wat Saket.

Longtails
It's sometimes easier to hire a long-tail boat (see Out & About) for heavily canalled areas like Thonburi.

Taxi

Taxis in Bangkok are plentiful but victims of traffic vagaries. Take the meter taxis – you don't have to barter (but be assertive in making sure the meter is turned on) and they're air-conditioned (good in a traffic jam). You pay a 35B flagfall, then 4.5B/km for trips between 2km and 12km, 5B/km between 13km and 20km and 5.5B/km over 20km; in a traffic jam you pay 1.25B a minute. Passengers pay all tolls.

Tuk-Tuks

These putt-putting little three-wheelers are best for short trips, preferably at night, when pollution probably won't sour your al-fresco trip. They're really only worth catching for the novelty appeal as they're not much cheaper than meter taxis. You have to bargain – 40B for a short hop is a fair price.

Motorcycle Taxi

A trip on a motorcycle taxi is guaranteed to be super-quick and (hopefully) death-defying. Short journeys cost around 20B.

Car & Motorcycle

You're either extremely patient or mad to drive in Bangkok. Even once you get somewhere, the parking situation is usually a nightmare. You'll pay around 16B/L for petrol.

Road Rules
Appearances may be deceiving, but there are road rules in Bangkok. The current government is having a major crackdown on motorists who break rules by driving on the wrong (right-hand) side of the road and not wearing seatbelts. Spice Girls fans note: it's illegal to drive with platform shoes.

Rental
Car hire starts at around 1500B per day, but the rate usually gets cheaper if you hire by the week or month. Rental companies include:

Avis (☎ 02 255 5300) 2/12 Th Witthayu, Pathumwan

Budget (☎ 02 552 8921) Bangkok International Airport

Driving Licence & Permit
You are required to have an International Driving Permit to drive in Bangkok.

Motoring Organisations
If you break down, you could try contacting Carworld Club (☎ 02 398 0170), which offers roadside assistance.

PRACTICAL INFORMATION

Climate & When to Go

The best time to visit Bangkok is during the cooler and drier months between November to February, though this time, as well as March and August, is the peak season, when it can be hard to find accommodation or get on a flight you want at short notice. Between April and May it's unbearably hot, while in September and October you'll probably have to wade your way through flooded streets. A much better way to splash around is during the Songkhran Festival, the famous Thai new year celebrations where everyone throws a lot of water around.

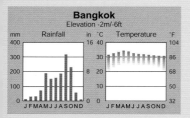

Bangkok
Elevation -2m/-6ft

Tourist Information

Tourist Information Abroad

The Tourist Authority of Thailand (TAT) has offices in these cities:

Australia & New Zealand
(☎ 02-9247 7549) 2nd fl, 75 Pitt St, Sydney, NSW 2000

UK
(☎ 020-7499 7679) 49 Albemarle St, London W1X 3FE

USA & Canada
(☎ 323-461-9814) 611 Nth Larchmont Blvd, 1st fl, Los Angeles, CA 90004

Local Tourist Information

You can get information and advice from TAT and Bangkok Tourist Bureau (BTB) offices. Tourist Police offices give limited advice but can help if you get in trouble. Beware of bogus tourist offices or officials purporting to be the real deal.

BTB (6, C1; ☎ 02 225 7612-5) 17/1 Th Phra Athit, Banglamphu

TAT (2, E7; ☎ 02 694 1222) 4 Th Ratchadamnoen Nok, Dusit

TAT (1, B5; ☎ 02 523 8972-3) Terminal 1, Bangkok International Airport

TAT (6, D3 or 6, C4; ☎ 02 272 4448) Chatukchak Weekend Market

Tourist Police (2, E4; ☎ 1155) Th Chakraphong, Banglamphu

Embassies

Australia
(3, J9; ☎ 02 287 2680) 37 Th Sathon Tai

Cambodia
(3, E9; ☎ 02 254 6630) 153 Th Ratchadamri

Canada
(3, G9; ☎ 02 636 0540) 15th fl, Abdulrahim Bldg, 990 Rama IV

Laos
(1, F5; ☎ 02 539 6667) 520/1-3 Soi 39, Th Ramkhamhaeng

Myanmar (Burma)
(3, J5; ☎ 02 233 2237) 132 Th Sathon Nua

New Zealand
(3, E12; ☎ 02 254 2530) 14th fl, All Seasons Place Bldg, 87 Th Witthayu

UK
(3, C11; ☎ 02 253 0191-9) 1031 Th Witthayu

USA
(3, E11;02 205 4000) 120-22 Th Witthayu

Money

Currency

The basic unit of Thai currency is the *baht*, made up of 100 *satang*. Notes come in denominations of

10B, 20B, 50B, 100B, 500B and 1000B, while coins come in 25 satang, 50 satang, 1B, 5B and 10B.

Travellers Cheques

It's better to change travellers cheques at banks, though you don't pay a commission if you change American Express cheques at its agent, SEA Tours (3, 7B), 4th fl, Siam Centre, Th Rama I.

Credit Cards

You'll have few problems using your credit card – especially if it's a Visa, MasterCard, Diners Club or AmEx – at most mid-range and top-end hotels and restaurants. For 24-hr card cancellations or assistance, call:

American Express	☎ 02 273 0022
Diners Club	☎ 02 238 2680
MasterCard	☎ 02 256 7326-7
Visa	☎ 02 256 7326-7

ATMs

Automatic Teller Machines are widespread and usually accept Cirrus, Plus, Maestro, JCB and Visa cards.

Changing Money

The banks offer the best rates for changing money. They're generally open Monday to Friday 10am to 4pm but some have currency exchange counters that operate 8am to 8pm.

Tipping

Tipping isn't normal in Thailand, but many mid-range and expensive restaurants add a 10% service charge to the bill.

Discounts

Kids, students and seniors generally pay the same prices as everyone, though particularly family-friendly attractions, like Siam Water Park, have kids' prices.

Student & Youth Cards

If you show your student card you can buy discounted Skytrain passes (but not single-trip tickets).

Seniors' Cards

You don't usually find seniors' discounts in Bangkok.

Travel Insurance

A policy covering theft, loss, medical expenses and compensation for cancellation or delays in your travel arrangements is highly recommended. If items are lost or stolen, make sure you get a police report or your insurer might not pay up.

Opening Hours

Businesses usually operate Monday to Friday 8.30am to 5pm and sometimes Saturday morning. Restaurants generally open daily from around 10am to 10pm, while shops in tourist areas open daily at 10am and shut between 7pm and 10pm. Most Chinatown businesses, and Chinese-run businesses in other parts of the city, close down during the lunar Chinese new year holiday (three days in February to March).

Public Holidays

Lunar holidays change each year – check the TAT Web site (e www .tat.or.th) for precise dates.

1 Jan	New Year 's Day
Jan-Mar	Magha Puja (lunar)
6 Apr	Chakri Day
Apr	Songkhran Festival (lunar)
5 May	Coronation Day
May	Visakha Puja (lunar)
Jul	Asalha Puja (lunar)
Jul	Khao Phansaa (lunar)
12 Aug	Queen's Birthay
23 Oct	Chulalongkorn Day
5 Dec	King's Birthay
10 Dec	Constitution Day

Time

Bangkok Standard Time is 7hrs ahead of GMT/UTC. At noon in Bangkok it's:

midnight in New York
9pm the previous day in Los Angeles
5am in London
7am in Johannesburg
3pm in Sydney
5pm in Auckland

Electricity

Electric currents in Thailand are 220V, 50 cycles. Most electrical wall outlets take the round, two-prong terminals, but some will take flat, two-bladed terminals and others will take both. It's easier to bring a converter from home than hunt down an electrical store in Bangkok.

Weights & Measures

Thailand uses the metric system, except when it comes to land measure, which is often quoted using the traditional system of *waa*, *ngaan* and *râi*. See also the conversion table on page 122.

Post

Thailand has an efficient national postal service. The main post office (3, H2) is on Th Charoen Krung, btw Sois 32 and 34. Two handy post offices are on Th Sukhumvit, near the corner of Soi 3, and Th Tani in Banglamphu; both have telecommunications offices. Some postal codes you might find handy include: Bangrak (10500), Khlong Toey (10110), Pathumwan (10330) and Ratchadamnoen (10200).

Postal Rates

You'll pay between 12B and 15B to send a postcard anywhere in the world, while aerograms will cost a flat 15B. Letter-writers will pay 17B to post to Australasia and Europe, and 19B to the Americas.

Opening Hours

The GPO is open from Monday to Saturday 8am to 8pm and Sunday and holidays 8am to 1pm, while post office agencies operate from Monday to Friday 8.30am to 5.30pm and Saturday 9am to noon.

Telephone

Phone booths are widespread. Red phones, taking coins, are for local calls; blue, also coin-operated, are for local and long-distance calls within Thailand; and green take phonecards. Local calls cost 1B for around 3mins.

Phonecards

You can buy phonecards at department stores and 7-Eleven shops. Local call cards are in 50B and 100B denominations and international cards come in 100B and 200B. Lonely Planet's eKno Communication Card, specifically aimed at travellers, provides competitive international calls (avoid using it for local calls), messaging services as well as free email. Log on to **e** www.ekno.lonelyplanet.com for information on joining and accessing the service.

Mobile Phones

You will need to arrange to use global roaming for your mobile phone before you leave home or you won't be able to use it in Bangkok.

Country & City Codes

All Thai phone numbers now have eight digits – even when you're calling within Bangkok, you must use the area code (☎ 02).

Thailand	☎ 66
Bangkok	☎ 02

Useful Numbers

Local Directory Inquiries	☎ 1133
International Directory Inquiries	☎ 100
International Operator	☎ 100
Reverse-Charge (collect)	☎ 100

International Direct Dial Codes

Dial ☎ 001 followed by:

Australia	☎ 61
Canada	☎ 1
Japan	☎ 81
New Zealand	☎ 64
South Africa	☎ 27
UK	☎ 44
USA	☎ 1

Electronic Resources

The Internet is hugely popular in Bangkok, with intense competition between Internet cafes pushing down access prices to around 1B per minute.

Internet Service Providers

If you're staying for a while, you might want to get a local account – the most reliable Thai ISPs include Loxinfo (☎ 02 263 8000), which offers temporary accounts, and Internet KSC (☎ 02 576 0899).

Internet Cafes

If you can't access the Internet from where you're staying, head to an Internet cafe. Banglamphu – especially on Th Khao San, Th Chakraphong and Th Rambutri – is crammed with Internet cafes offering the most competitive rates in Bangkok, sometimes as low as 0.5B a minute. Many shopping centres, such as MBK and Panthip Plaza, have an 'entertainment floor', with Internet cafes charging around 1B per minute. You could also try this Thai Internet cafe chain with reliable access and good coffee:

Coffee World

(3, D13; ☎ 252 0253) b/w sois 3 & 5, Th Sukhumvit; [e] info@coffee-world.com, www.coffee-world.com; open 8am-10pm; 100B for 80mins

Coffee World

(3, H6; ☎ 02 634 3140) 144/3-4 Th Silom; [e] info@coffee-world.com, www.coffee-world.com; open 8am-10pm; 100B for 80mins

Useful Sites

Lonely Planet's website ([e] www.lonelyplanet.com) offers a speedy link to many of Thailand's websites. Others to try include:

Bangkok Metro
[e] www.bkkmetro.com

Bangkok Post
[e] www.bangkokpost.net

Bangkok Thailand Today
[e] www.bangkok.thailandtoday.com

The Nation
[e] www.nationmultimedia.com

Tourism Authority of Thailand
[e] www.tat.or.th

CitySync

CitySync Bangkok is the Lonely Planet digital guide for Palm OS hand-held devices, allowing quick searches, sorting and bookmarking of hundreds of Bangkok's attractions, clubs, hotels, restaurants and much more, all pinpointed on scrollable street maps. Buy or demo CitySync Bangkok at [e] www.citysync.com.

Doing Business

Bangkok's big hotels have well-equipped business centres, where you can arrange to use workstations and fax services, hire meeting rooms or find a translator.

If you are looking for secretarial services, you could try Girl Friday Business & Secretarial Services

(☎ 02 635 0182), 191/5 Soi Seuksa Withaya, Th Silom.

Associations like the Australian-Thai Chamber of Commerce (☎ 02 210 0217-8), American Chamber of Commerce (☎ 02 251 9266-7) and the British Chamber of Commerce (☎ 02 651 5350-3) can help you with contacts and advice. If you're in the import/export game, you should get in touch with the Thai Chamber of Commerce (☎ 02 662 18060).

Newspapers & Magazines

Bangkok has two English-language broadsheets, the more serious *Bangkok Post* and *The Nation*. Bookazine bookshops have the best range of foreign newspapers and magazines, though you can usually pick up a copy of *Time*, *The Economist* and the *International Herald Tribune* at newsagents in tourist areas. If you plan to hit the restaurants and nightspots, a copy of the excellent listings mag *Bangkok Metro* is a worthy investment. The free *BKK Magazine* is also good for nightlife and restaurant reviews. Of the gay streetpress, *Gay Max* and *Thai Guys* seem to be the best.

Radio

Bangkok has over 70 radio stations, many of them broadcasting in Thai and English. Gold FMX (95.5FM) and Star FM (102.5FM) have bilingual DJs playing rock, R&B and pop. For easy listening, Thai-style, tune into 87.5FM, which plays pop and *lûuk thûng* (Thai country music with a high croon factor).

TV

Of the five TV stations, two (channels 5 and 7) are owned by the military, two (channels 9 and 11) by the government and one (channel 3) is in private hands. They show the usual mix of zany game shows, highly amusing soap operas and news programs. Cable TV in Thailand is run by UBC, which has channels like MTV Asia, BBC World and CNN.

Photography & Video

Print and slide film and VHS video cassettes are widely available and inexpensive. There are many film-processing labs, with good rates, throughout the city.

Thailand uses the PAL video system, which is compatible with Europe (except France) and Australia. Some video shops sell NTSC format tapes, compatible with the USA and Japan.

Health

Immunisations

You don't really need to get any vaccinations, unless you plan to travel outside Bangkok, but it's wise to make sure your tetanus and polio boosters are up to date. Although there is no risk of yellow fever in Bangkok, you will need proof of vaccination if you're coming from a yellow-fever infected area, like Africa or parts of South America.

Precautions

It's not uncommon to get a mild case of 'Bangkok belly' as your body adjusts to a new diet, but to avoid problems, keep a few things in mind. Don't drink Bangkok tap water, nor use it to clean your teeth, but it's OK to drink the water served in restaurants and hotels as it's purified. Avoid drinking chipped ice, which is often unhygienic – stick to ice cubes. Beware of ice cream that may have melted and been refrozen, as well as shellfish, like mussels and clams, and undercooked mince. If a place looks clean and well-run and the owner also looks clean and healthy, the food is probably safe; often places that are busy with travellers or locals will be fine.

Malaria is not a problem in Bangkok but you should always try to avoid getting bitten by mosquitoes, as there are occasional reports of dengue fever in Bangkok. The mosquito that transmits the virus is most active during the day.

Some people find it difficult to adjust to the heat and humidity – make sure you drink lots of fluids and take it easy on the first few days. If you do get Bangkok belly, be vigilant about fluid replacement.

Like anywhere else, practise the usual precautions when it comes to sex; condoms are widely available from chemists and supermarkets.

Insurance & Medical Treatment

Travel insurance is advisable to cover any medical treatment you may need while in Bangkok. Medical treatment is reasonably priced and of a good standard.

Medical Services

Hospitals with 24hr accident and emergency departments include:

BNH Hospital
(3, H8; ☎ 02632 0577-9) 9/1 Soi Convent, Th Silom

Bumrungrad Hospital
(3, B13; ☎ 02 667 1000) 33 Soi 3, Th Sukhumvit

Samitivej Hospital
(1, G4; ☎ 02 392 0011-9) 133 Soi 49, Th Sukhumvit

Dental Services

If you chip a tooth or require emergency treatment then head to the dental clinic at major hospitals like Bumrungrad (see Medical Services earlier).

Pharmacies

The British chemist chain Boots has many Bangkok outlets with long opening hours – you could try branches at the Emporium (4, D4; btw Sois 22 and 24, Th Sukhumvit), Siam Discovery Centre (3, B7; cnr Th Phayathai and Th Phra Ram 1) or in Banglamphu (6, D3; 59-63 Th Khao San).

Toilets

The best places to find public toilets are department stores, cinemas and tourist sites. Though most toilets you'll see will be of the Western sit-down variety, you may come across squat toilets. Next to these toilets is a bucket of water with a plastic bowl – use the water to wash yourself on the toilet and then later flush waste into the septic system. Never flush paper down these toilets. Often sit-down toilets have a bucket full of used toilet paper next to them – a sign that you should do the same.

Safety Concerns

Considering its size, Bangkok is a relatively safe city. But you should be smart: don't wander down dark alleyways alone and always protect against theft (use a hotel safe and conceal valuables).

Be wary of friendly strangers offering cigarettes, food and drink, as some people have been known to mix heavy sedatives in them – men have often been victims of drugged food and drinks from women in bars or prostitutes, though women should be just as vigilant. There may seem to be plenty of drugs like heroin, amphetamines, ecstasy, marijuana and hallucinogens around, but buying, selling or possessing them is illegal. Touts are mostly more irritable than dangerous, but don't take anything they say seriously and instead check things out yourself. See Shopping for information on gem scams.

Lost Property
For lost items on a bus call ☎ 184, on Skytrain call ☎ 02 617 7300 and on Chao Phraya River Express boats call ☎ 02 225 3002-3.

Keeping Copies
Make photocopies of all your important documents, keep some with you, separate from the originals, and leave a copy at home. You can also store details of documents in Lonely Planet's free online Travel Vault, password-protected and accessible worldwide. See e www.ekno.lonelyplanet.com.

Emergency Numbers

Ambulance	☎ 191
Fire	☎ 199
Police	☎ 191
Tourist Police	☎ 1155

Women Travellers

Bangkok is not particularly dangerous for women and they'll probably receive less unwanted attention than in other Asian countries like India and Indonesia. But women would be wise not to travel alone at night, especially in tuk-tuks, and should stay at a hotel or guesthouse with good security and ensure their rooms are secure.

Tampons and the contraceptive pill are easily available from chemists like Boots, though the range of brands is not extensive. Supermarkets have reasonable stocks of tampons.

Gay & Lesbian Travellers

As you'll soon notice, Thai culture is incredibly tolerant of homosexuality, but public displays of affection, whether you're gay or straight, are no-nos. As homosexuality is generally accepted (but not really talked about), there isn't a gay political movement as such. But there is the 'pink triangle' of Th Silom, Th Surawong and Th Sathon, an area with loads of bars, cafes and saunas. The lesbian scene is much more low-key and not centred in the entertainment districts.

Information & Organisations
Dreaded Ned's website (e www.dreadedned.com) is an excellent place to get the lowdown on Bangkok's gay scene, as are the street mags like Gay Max. You could also get in touch with the lesbian group Anjaree (☎ 02 2435 7348) or the Thai chapter of the gay Long Yang Club (☎ 02 2677 6965).

Senior Travellers

Bangkok can be a difficult place to get around, with plenty of broken footpaths, stairs and crazy drivers to contend with when crossing roads, not to mention energy-sapping humidity. You won't have much luck finding seniors discounts or organisations but you'll probably be shown great respect, like Thai seniors.

Disabled Travellers

Movement around the streets of Bangkok can be a complete nightmare – there are few sloping kerbs or wheelchair ramps, and many streets are best crossed via stair-heavy pedestrian crossings.

Some disabled travellers recommend hiring a taxi or private car and driver to see the sights, rather than taking tours, though it can be difficult fitting wheelchairs in the taxi boot. Five Skytrain stations – Asok, Chong Nonsi, Mo Chit, On Nut and Siam – have elevators. You can travel for free from these stations if you show your disabled association membership. Some hotel chains, like Amari and Banyan Tree, are particularly aware of the needs of disabled travellers.

Information & Organisations

Association of the Physically Handicapped of Thailand (☎ 02 951 0569) is a good source of information, as is Disabled Peoples International (☎ 02 583 3021).

Language

Thailand's official language is Thai. The dialect from Central Thailand has been adopted as the lingua franca, though regional dialects are still spoken. Thai is a tonal language, so a single syllable may be altered by different tones. In Central Thai there are five tones, indicated by accents: low – á, level or mid – a (no acccent), falling – â, high – à and rising – ǎ. Written Thai is read from left to right. It's quite complex to learn, so if you'll only be in Bangkok for a short time it's better to try to pick up spoken Thai.

Something that can be confusing for travellers is the transliteration of Thai script into English – some signs will call a street Th Rajadamnoen Nok, but we'll call it Th Ratchadamnoen Nok. Both are correct – the problem is that there's no transliteration system that has satisfied everyone, so everyone uses different ones. In this book, we've used the most common practice or adopted the Roman names that hotels, restaurants etc use.

Basics

Greetings/Hello.	sàwàt-dii
Goodbye.	laa kàwn
How are you?	sàbai dii rěu?
I'm fine.	sàbai dii
Please.	kàrúnaa
Thank you.	khàwp khun
Excuse me.	khǎw thôht
What's your name?	khun chêu àrai?
My name is ...	phǒm chêu ... (men)
	di-chǎn chêu ... (women)

I understand.	khâo jai
I don't understand.	mâi khâo jai
What do you call this in Thai?	nîi phaasǎa thairîak wâa àrai?

How much?	thâo raí?
Help!	chûay dûay!
Stop!	yùt!
I'm lost.	chǎn lǒng thaang

Time & Numbers

What's the time?	kii mohng láew?
today	wan níi
tomorrow	phrûng níi
yesterday	mêua waan

1	nèung
2	sǎwng
3	sǎam
4	sìi
5	hâa
6	hòk
7	jèt
8	pàet
9	kâo
10	sìp
11	sìp-èt
12	sìp-sǎwng
13	sìp-sǎam
20	yîi-sìp
21	yîi-sìp-èt
22	yîi-sìp-sǎwng
30	sǎam-sìp
40	sìi-sìp
50	hâa-sìp
100	ráwy
200	sǎwng ráwy
1000	phan

one million	láan

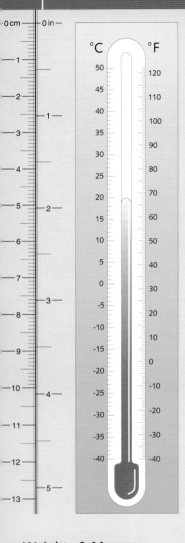

Conversion Table

Clothing Sizes
Measurements approximate only; try before you buy.

Women's Clothing

Aust/NZ	8	10	12	14	16	18
Europe	36	38	40	42	44	46
Japan	5	7	9	11	13	15
UK	8	10	12	14	16	18
USA	6	8	10	12	14	16

Women's Shoes

Aust/NZ	5	6	7	8	9	10
Europe	35	36	37	38	39	40
France only	35	36	38	39	40	42
Japan	22	23	24	25	26	27
UK	3½	4½	5½	6½	7½	8½
USA	5	6	7	8	9	10

Men's Clothing

Aust/NZ	92	96	100	104	108	112
Europe	46	48	50	52	54	56
Japan	S		M	M		L
UK	35	36	37	38	39	40
USA	35	36	37	38	39	40

Men's Shirts (Collar Sizes)

Aust/NZ	38	39	40	41	42	43
Europe	38	39	40	41	42	43
Japan	38	39	40	41	42	43
UK	15	15½	16	16½	17	17½
USA	15	15½	16	16½	17	17½

Men's Shoes

Aust/NZ	7	8	9	10	11	12
Europe	41	42	43	44½	46	47
Japan	26	27	27.5	28	29	30
UK	7	8	9	10	11	12
USA	7½	8½	9½	10½	11½	12½

Weights & Measures

Weight
1kg = 2.2lb
1lb = 0.45kg
1g = 0.04oz
1oz = 28g

Volume
1 litre = 0.26 US gallons
1 US gallon = 3.8 litres
1 litre = 0.22 imperial gallons
1 imperial gallon = 4.55 litres

Length & Distance
1 inch = 2.54cm
1cm = 0.39 inches
1m = 3.3ft = 1.1yds
1ft = 0.3m
1km = 0.62 miles
1 mile = 1.6km

lonely planet

Lonely Planet is the world's most successful independent travel information company with offices in Australia, the US, UK and France. With a reputation for comprehensive, reliable travel information, Lonely Planet is a print and electronic publishing leader, with over 650 titles and 22 series catering for travellers' individual needs.

At Lonely Planet we believe that travellers can make a positive contribution to the countries they visit – if they respect their host communities and spend their money wisely. Since 1986 a percentage of the income from books has been donated to aid and human rights projects.

www.lonelyplanet.com

For news, views and free subscriptions to print and email newsletters, and a full list of LP titles, click on Lonely Planet's award-winning website.

On the Town

A romantic escape to Paris or a mad shopping dash through New York City, the locals' secret bars or a city's top attractions – whether you have 24 hours to kill or months to explore, Lonely Planet's On the Town products will give you the low-down.

Condensed guides are ideal pocket guides for when time is tight. Their quick-view maps, full-colour layout and opinionated reviews help short-term visitors target the top sights and discover the very best eating, shopping and entertainment options a city has to offer.

For more indepth coverage, **City guides** offer insights into a city's character and cultural background as well as providing broad coverage of where to eat, stay and play. **CitySync**, a digital guide for your handheld unit, allows you to reference stacks of opinionated, well-researched travel information. Portable and durable **City Maps** are perfect for locating those back-street bars or hard-to-find local haunts.

'Ideal for a generation of fast movers.'

– Gourmet Traveller on Condensed guides

Condensed Guides

- Amsterdam
- Athens
- Bangkok
- Barcelona
- Beijing (March 2003)
- Boston
- Chicago
- Dublin
- Florence (May 2003)
- Frankfurt
- Hong Kong
- Las Vegas (May 2003)
- London
- Los Angeles
- Madrid (March 2003)
- New Orleans (March 2003)
- New York City
- Paris
- Prague
- Rome
- San Francisco
- Singapore
- Sydney
- Tokyo
- Venice
- Washington, DC

index

See also separate indexes for Places to Eat (p. 126), Places to Stay (p. 127), Shops (p. 127) and Sights with map references (p. 128).

PLACES TO EAT

PLACES TO STAY

SHOPS

sights – quick index